Up, Up
AND
Away

**One Man's Struggle to Wage
His Own Personal Ground War**

Richard Corbett

Up, Up and Away:
One Man's Struggle to Wage His Own Personal Ground War
Copyright © 2013 Richard Corbett

All rights reserved. No part of this book may be reproduced (except for inclusion in reviews), disseminated or utilized in any form or by any means, electronic or mechanical, including photocopying, recording, or in any information storage and retrieval system, or the Internet/World Wide Web without written permission from the author or publisher.

For more information:
rick.d.corbett@gmail.com

Up, Up and Away:
One Man's Struggle to Wage His Own Personal Ground War
Richard Corbett

Acknowledgments

It's amazing how during my brief run at Modesto Flight Center I came across so many great people. I will highlight a handful, understanding that I can't acknowledge everybody.

First I would like to thank Julie, for her incredible fortitude during those trying years we ran the flight school. She exhibited a positive attitude, kept my spirits up, and was my advocate for what we had to deal with. Thanks so much for helping me out!

To my mom and dad—well, you brought me around airports early on and got me smelling jet fumes, hooking me on airplanes and airports. Thanks for all the support and your encouraging words.

To Brandon—thank you for your help at the flight school. You put yourself out selflessly and I appreciate the assistance, though I didn't say it enough.

To Tony—wow, that was a ride, huh? I want to thank you for your support and will try to keep the flight school going as long as we can. Maybe next time I'll let you run things!

To those flight instructors I've worked with in the past, too numerous to list—all I can say is thanks for all the support and patience in building my flying skills and proficiencies.

To Michael Dye—thanks, brother, for your candid discussions on everything aviation and business. You were a great supporter in this entire process, all the way to the shutdown. Always kept a positive attitude unless you saw or heard something ridiculous....then you gave me an earful on how crazy things were. No one said it better than you: "It is what it is."

I would also like to thank Karen Cole and Bruce Brager of Rainbow Writing, Inc. and Elise Vaz of Arbor Books for their editorial work and assistance on this book. I am deeply appreciative of your help to allow me to take on this project and to be able to express the events that occurred, and how this book could help prevent them from happening to others in the business community.

To the community of Modesto, which came out in support of Modesto Flight Center—I thank you all. I tried to overcome the issues and bring services to our community. Some folks obviously didn't like that. But for those who were on our side, many thanks!

Introduction	My Background	3
Chapter One:	The Flight School	17
Chapter Two:	The Fueling Farm Idea	25
Chapter Three:	The Real Process Begins	39
Chapter Four:	Early Staff Work	47
Chapter Five:	The Airport Advisory Committee	55
Chapter Six:	Environmental Issues	85
Chapter Seven:	Hey, Gang! Let's do an Environmental Study!	97
Chapter Eight:	Personal Financial Statement	111
Chapter Nine:	The Lawyers Jump In Full Force	119
Chapter Ten:	Meanwhile, Back at the Environmental Study	147
Chapter Eleven:	Summaries of Process and Progress	155
Chapter Twelve:	More About the Environmental Study	181
Chapter Thirteen:	The Last Hurrah	197
Chapter Fourteen:	The Process in Retrospect	205
Chapter Fifteen:	Would I do it Again?	211
Appendix		215
Citations		219

2

Introduction
My Background

This story begins in August 2007, when I bought a flight school based at the Modesto, California, airport. Giving back to the aviation industry and the people who wanted to be part of the industry was one of my life goals. I'd longed for this opportunity and thought my wish was coming true. Be careful what you wish for, the old saying goes; you might get it.

This story also begins with my growing up in Oakland, with my mother and father both working in the commercial airline industry.

I had three life goals. I wanted to serve in the military, particularly as a pilot; I wanted to work for a major airline; and I wanted to give back, to help others share my love of flying. Through Air Force Reserve Officer Training Corps (ROTC), ten years of service in the Air Force, and service since 2001 as a pilot in the United States Air Force Reserve, I readily achieved my first goal.

My second goal was to work for a major airline as a pilot. I achieved this goal in 2006, when I joined JetBlue Airways. I've flown for them ever since.

My third goal was to give back to others. I thought I achieved that goal in 2007, when I purchased a flight school—the Modesto Flight Center, which also provided general aviation services. This interest expanded into the desire to open a fueling center for general aviation at the Modesto Airport. The airport, a medium-sized general aviation facility, had only one fueling facility. I thought the center needed competition and this was a service I could supply. It was there things got interesting, and in many ways I mean this in the traditional Chinese sense of being a curse.

This book tells the story of my adventures with aviation fueling and my unexpected and unwelcome adventures with local government and small versus big business. I'm not sure how to describe this book—maybe as David versus Goliath, where David wanted to farm alongside Goliath but the big guy wasn't inclined to be cooperative. And unlike the real Goliath, who certainly didn't hide his apparent power or intent, this Goliath preferred to work behind the scenes.

It is a political melodrama, a story of how political influence trumps logic, and, as sometimes happens, self-interest; a comedy of errors; a story of misbehaving large business at the expense of small business. I have in my notes the line, "Bleeding a small businessman for the sake of larger business." Readers will see how true this is, or whatever else you might choose as a theme.

Goliath won this one, but this book may help others do better next time. As an example I quote a paragraph from a letter prepared several months into the process, which included a summary of the applicability of the Modesto political situation to other similar communities, and the relevance of my story elsewhere.

In my experience this type of behavior is common in communities across the country where a city or county attempts to operate its airport in a vacuum, with the belief that the best course of action for dealing with a proposer like MFC is a political one, which can effectively bar competition and promote discriminatory practices. However this is exactly the type of behavior that is frowned upon by the FAA, which looks at an airport's management as the on-site entity responsible for representing the FAA's ultimate interests and avoiding discriminatory practices with respect to commercial aeronautical operators. After all the FAA is really the owner of the airport's infrastructure, and the city is the custodian.

Readers will have a fair amount of quoted documents to read, including FAA regulations—the laws governing operations of airports. This is part of what I followed in the book, to let readers read the words of the participants—some of which I had available at the time, some of which I didn't—and let them make up their own minds.

This is real evidence, facts in support of my contentions, and not just the printed sound of my own voice. I added my own analysis—what I thought then and what things look like now. Again readers can make up their own minds about what the documents say and about my own personal conclusions.

This is an interesting story, a tale worth telling and, I'm sure, worth reading. At the end the readers will learn whether I think this was a story worth living, what I might have done differently, and whether I would do something like this again if I could.

Though it may not seem like it, I'm not out to settle scores. I am out to tell my story and show what can happen when one takes on any power structure, local or otherwise. I'm out to provide a warning for others—by no means those who might want to take on the government and entrenched businesses of Modesto, California, but all those who might look to challenge an entrenched business or political power structure.

The facts are as I remember them. I conducted backup research when possible to get details I might not have known and general information. But keep this in mind: as I said, the facts are as I remember them. Things such as conversations I had with one other person can't be documented unless there is correspondence to confirm and a response saying "confirmed." Some of the one-on-one conversations could and would not be confirmed. Since some of the parties do not come out well, it would not be in their immediate self-interest, aside from under oath in a court of law, to confirm these conversations.

It takes a very honest man or woman to confirm—outside of sworn testimony, without any hedging—a conversation that makes him or her look bad. "Yes, I told Mr. Corbett the city is out to screw him" is a very unlikely response. Far more likely, since we are dealing with human beings, is something of out-and-out denial like, "I think Mr. Corbett is misinterpreting what I said." It is much better to claim a person misunderstood than to call someone a liar.

Remember that the stated meanings of the facts presented in this book are my own interpretations. Though I can't cite specific examples at the moment, one or two facts leading to a conclusion might have been misinterpreted. I've tried to be as objective as possible. More facts make the conclusion far more certain. However I stand by my interpretation and that the facts above, those not reported in documents, are as accurate as I remember them.

More about the particular conditions in Modesto later; now a few words about what government in general can do for business. The exact degree of desirable government involvement in the business world within its jurisdiction will depend a lot on the politics of the speaker—which we hope adapts to circumstances. Just read any national newspaper for the continuing debate over government involvement in and regulation of business.

But one thing we might agree on is that whatever the extent of government involvement, there is a need for basic fairness. The playing field should be as level as possible, though this will never be fully achieved. Rules should be clear and open. Each business should have an equal chance of success, though success will depend on the resources and basic skills people in the business bring to the table as well as their desire to do the job. *Skills* means not just the ability to do the job but the perception and foresight to identify a need and to find a job worth doing.

I thought I brought my abilities to the job, and I know I brought the interest. I had identified a job that needed doing: a second fueling alternative for pilots at the Modesto airport. I brought what I hoped was a sense of fairness to the task, meaning that had the situation been reversed I would not have tried to destroy Sky Trek. I thought I would find a level playing field for my business where I would succeed or fail on my own. I considered myself no more entitled to protection from the general economy than anyone else. I sought no protection from the normally great risks of opening or expanding a small business. But at the risk of sounding a little obsessive, I expected a level playing field. I thought the general economy was the only outside factor I had to worry about.

This was where I was most wrong.

The Project

In May of 2008, at the request of Modesto city official Jerome Thiele, the airport manager, I prepared a summary of the project. I think it is useful to let everyone reading this book know exactly what I was planning—my goal in this whole story.

> Over the last few months planning for a fuel farm operation at the Modesto Flight Center have [sic] been underway. While most of the information that will be included in this memo has been talked about or included in other departments the request has been made to have a complete physical description of the project with appropriate backups.
> The proposal includes both an Avgas and JetA component situated in the same general area of the Modesto Airport.
> The area proposed for the fuel farm is directly in front of the Modesto Flight Center offices on Tioga Dr. on the west side of the airport. The area, through GPS locator, has been OK'd by the FAA as being suitable for the project.
> The fuel farm will consist of one 12,000 gallon Avgas tank (equipped to handle self-serve only) and one 12,000 gallon JetA (equipped to handle self-serve and refueler reloading). Credit card processing equipment will be located between the two tanks (along with the hose reels and related equipment). Power for the operation will be run underground from the Modesto Flight Centers hanger just to the north of the MFC offices. Phone lines (for credit card authorization) will also be run from the fuel farm to the MPC offices. A Phillips sign will be pole mounted with the fuel tanks pad

area.

The fuel farm will be mounted to a concrete pad that meets city/county code, approximately 20' by 70' with tanks sitting in line "nose to nose." The area chosen for the pad is the tie-down area currently leased by MFC with exceptional access from the Westside taxiways.

The fuel tanks (Avgas and JetA) will be manufactured by Garsite Tanks per the spec listed on the attached quote sheet. The JetA tank will be similarly constructed by Garsite. We will also provide the Modesto Flight Center with a JetA refueling truck, the model and side yet to be determined…

This sounds somewhat like the self-service gas stations most of us use for our cars. Actually it is somewhat safer, with the fuel tanks above ground. The concrete pad would protect the soil and groundwater from any fuel leakage. The planned fueling center would be something like the fourteenth facility installed in California to use this technology, and so far there had been no environmental or safety problems, so the technology was neither particularly new nor untried. It was newer than what was used by my opponent in this story, Sky Trek. As far as I know, this has not changed. The need for expanded fuel facilities for general aviation throughout the country also has not changed.

Earlier in 2010 an official from the Tennessee Department of Transportation was quoted in an article in the *Nashville Business Journal* as saying "many airports are asking for assistance to purchase unmanned fuel pumps that accept credit cards, helping them cut expenses and add conveniences for flyers.

And while it isn't quite a gas war, the said airports are keeping their gas prices as low as possible." He further said that many airports are also seeking help to extend their runways to 5,000 feet, which he said is a new "magic number" for the insurers of larger corporate planes.[1]

Two years ago, about the time serious obstacles were arising in my project, *The Denver Business Journal* wrote this about the fuel situation for generation aviation:

> Increased fuel costs and rising airplane rental costs are grounding many recreational pilots and small business owners across the state—and that's bad news for small airports.
>
> Metro-area general aviation airport managers say revenue dropped between 15 percent and 30 percent in the first quarter due to rising fuel costs.
>
> When airport revenue declines, capital improvement projects are put on hold, employees are laid off, and takeoffs and landings are reduced.
>
> Fuel prices in the general aviation industry have increased roughly 30 percent in the last year, according to TAC Air, an aviation fuel supplier at **Centennial Airport**.[2]

So both these business publications reported a problem with fuel prices. Modesto Airport should have welcomed a situation that would've lowered fuel prices at the airport and made the airport more competitive with other general aviation centers.

How did I get involved in this whole situation? What brought me to this point?

I've always been around airports; I've always been around

airplanes. This being so it stands to reason that I wanted to get into aviation. When I was a child, I would go to the Oakland International Airport to see where my parents worked. In the beginning they worked for Transamerica Airlines, a once-vibrant carrier that had multiple types of airframes—different types of airplanes allowing them to serve a wide variety of customers. Transamerica began under another name in 1947, flying DC-3 propeller airplanes—remarkable aircraft, but even then those were only older planes. After a forty-year existence, including work as a scheduled carrier and charter service, the airline was dissolved in 1986.

My visits to the airport moved across the bay to San Francisco. My mother worked in various departments at United Airlines and my stepfather worked as an inspector. This time frame was from the mid-1980s to around the time I graduated high school in 1991.

Not knowing what I wanted to do at that time other than fly, I decided to go into the Air Force Reserve. For those of you who are not sure, the Reserve is the backup force—though the wars in Iraq and Afghanistan show this backup can be crucial—directly administered by the federal government. The National Guard is a collection of state forces that can be mobilized by the federal government. Both forces are required to meet the same training standards as the regular military. I chose the Air Force Reserve.

I requested from the recruiter a flying job like a loadmaster supervising cargo on an airplane or something that would allow me to be near airplanes and/or fly as a crewmember. I ended up as an air transportation specialist, which was far from a flying job, though it gave me valuable background.

I guess I should consider it a starting point. This got me

closer to what I wanted to do and motivated me to move on quickly from that position.

Basic training and technical school were completed in 1991 and the beginning of 1992. I returned to my parents's house to attend college. My best option to fly was to enroll in the United States Air Force (USAF) Reserve Officer Training Corps (ROTC) at California State University in Sacramento.

I attended Delta College's general education courses in Stockton, California, and transferred to San Jose State University to finish my BA in behavior sciences. Before finishing my degree, regulations required me to give up my USAF reserve enlisted position from my junior year through graduation.

In 1996 I put in my "dream sheet"—my request for assignment after commissioning: pilot and then navigator. But back then pilot positions were somewhat scarce, and so I ended up with a navigator job.

Now, there is nothing wrong with being a navigator. This is valuable background, knowing how to direct where the plane goes as well as how to steer it while getting there. However, when you desire to be a pilot, it is a speed bump of sorts. It took me time to get through navigator training—over a year at two locations. The first phase took place in Pensacola, Florida. At least as far as training went it was a blast!

While I was in Pensacola, there wasn't anything like flying in a T-34C single-engine turbine plane. This was a turboprop version of the original piston engine T-34, which first flew in 1948. The T-34 was already a veteran airplane by the time I flew one but was sufficiently designed so it is only now being replaced as a trainer.

The bubble canopy, providing a near-360-degree view of the sky, was fantastic. I almost feel like I was in action in World

War II. This plane provided new pilots with the opportunity to develop their flying skills. It also produced the ample enjoyment necessary for sustaining interest in flying. Basically it was sheer fun.

To add to my pleasure, I lived on the beach, three doors down from the famous Flora-Bama bar, named because its western wall was all of six feet from the Florida-Alabama border. I was sorry to hear the bar was nearly totally wrecked by Hurricane Ivan in 2004 but am happy to hear it is being rebuilt. Nothing like the mullet toss events every summer!

After finishing the first phase of my flight training, I had to decide whether to stay in Pensacola and try for the fighter/bomber track or go to Randolph Air Force base in Texas to fly heavier aircraft such as transports and radar planes, known as *heavies*. My thought process was that I wanted the pilot job, and the most efficient way to get it would be to do the heavy track (shorter time) and apply for a pilot position.

I moved on to Randolph and flew in the T-43, a modified Boeing 737-200, as a navigator trainer. I finished in late 1997 and had to decide what aircraft to fly. I chose the E-3 airborne warning and control system (AWACS). This aircraft serves as both an early warning radar and a fighter control.

Some would say that was insane due to the monotonous flying and long duration of missions. But again, at the time I thought: how can I apply for a pilot position in the quickest and most efficient manner? Go for the airplane that would most swiftly provide me the opportunity to advance from being a navigator.

So I stayed in the E-3 program, stationed at Tinker AFB in Oklahoma, until December of 1999, when an assignment popped up for a navigator to work as a mission planner for the

U-2 spy plane at Beale AFB, California. That was convenient. I was married, and my wife, Julie, was living in California while I was Tinker AFB. The move would put us a lot closer together.

I applied and got the assignment as a first lieutenant, which was a first. Typical rank for a mission planner for the U-2 was senior major. The assignment was incredibly interesting, to say the least. Not getting into specifics—the U-2 is an intelligence asset, after all—it was satisfying to be part of such an important mission. Again, though this was still not the pilot spot I wanted, it gave me more valuable experience.

Next I began trying to be assigned a pilot job in the Air Force Reserve at Travis AFB, which was located over an hour from Beale AFB. I was able to obtain an interview with the KC-10 tanker squadron, and after a squadron and wing interview board I was selected to go to pilot training. But there was a problem: I still had several years left on my initial navigator commitment. I had to request a program called Palace Chase to allow my early exit not only from active duty but from the remaining years on my navigator commitment. I didn't want to leave the regular military, but Palace Chase was the best and most rapid way to achieve my goal of being a pilot. Palace Chase would also still allow the military to take advantage of my skills, though in a different area of the total force.

The Palace Chase process was a bit tedious, but I had solid support from my supervisors all the way up to the wing commander at Beale. (Perhaps I thus got too used to assuming that decisions makers would be supportive, or at least objective, on any approval process, and that all I had to do was do my current job and make a good case for what I wanted.) Palace Chase was approved in rapid fashion. Phew!

In July 2001 I separated from active duty. On August 1,

2001, I was a reservist again and heading to USAF pilot training at Laughlin AFB, Texas. Pilot training would last for a year. I would then return to Travis to train and fly the KC-10 Extender, a modified DC-10 used for refueling other aircraft in-flight, carrying cargo and hauling passengers.

I've been in the Air Force Reserve ever since. I fly worldwide missions covering virtually every continent, enjoying various cultures as well as gaining valuable flying experience. From Alice Springs, Australia, to Frankfurt, Germany, and from Bali, Indonesia, to Diego Garcia in the middle of the Indian Ocean, I've traveled the world more times over than you could even imagine!

Promotion in the military, to divert for a moment, comes in two ways. You can ask to be placed into a position that requires you to earn your promotion or be promoted and then locate the job appropriate to your rank. For higher positions the promotion can come with the assignment. All military promotions and assignments, in any service, require the consent of the Senate. But except for the highest ranks and positions, such as the four-star general commanding American and allied troops in Afghanistan, the process is routine.

In 2005 I got a call from JetBlue Airways asking me to come in for an interview, which I attended. The interview went well and I was notified not long afterward that I would be hired by JetBlue. I started training on March 31, 2006 as a first officer on an Airbus A-320 and finished training a month later. I was based in New York City initially but eventually made my way back to Long Beach, California, where I am currently based.

Chapter One
The Flight School

The introduction explains how I got into flying. But now, how is this all related to my flight school and to the proposed fueling facility—the subject of this story?

Flight training has existed since the beginning of powered flight. Orville Wright trained pilots, probably starting with showing Wilbur how to operate the flyer. The first formal flight school was opened by the Wright Brothers in 1910 in Alabama. This school wasn't financially successful; the Wrights were apparently better at inventing and developing than at running a business. But the idea of formal flight training stuck around. I jumped into the field about a century later.

I've always had an entrepreneurial itch, since almost as far back as I had a desire to fly. My wife and I opened a franchise tanning salon back in December 2003. This was a venture she was interested in, and we went for it. We still own it to this day. Once you begin to realize how amazing it is to own a business and manage it, it becomes part of you. You are in control; you are responsible. In many ways this is like flying. There are pains and annoyances that one must endure and there are great business risks, but overall there is a strong satisfaction associated with business ownership.

Back in late 2006, I was looking through the *Trade-A-Plane* paper, a journal for the general aviation industry, and was skimming the "business opportunities" section of the classified ads. I noticed a flight school/FBO (fixed based operator with ground facilities—the primary provider, or one of the primary providers, of services to general aviation at a specific airport) for sale in northern California, and I was intrigued.

I asked my wife, "Wouldn't it be fun to own our own flight school and give back to the aviation community what I have accomplished?" She agreed, and I inquired about the business through the posted contact. I contacted the owners and set up a meeting.

I was told it was Modesto Flight Center in Modesto, California. This was a business that had been around for twenty-five years. One of the two founders/owners had been killed in a plane crash a few months earlier, with a businessman passenger, in a home-built aircraft. Larry Askew, the other owner, had decided to get out of the business end of the flight center. An August 2007 article in the *Modesto Bee* implied as much. In it he said he was ready to let the next generation take over.

Askew wanted to stay on as a pilot and became chief instructor for the school. Reading between the lines, it seemed clear Askew had wanted to get out of the business end even before his partner was killed. This was good timing for me, as I wanted to get in.

At our meeting we discussed the business. I liked the prospects and tried to see great value in the company. I saw potential, growth, and a way to give back.

So I contacted a business loan company that told me the business could be United States Small Business Administration (SBA) approved. After a lengthy process—I seem to have a predilection for things that take time—with success so much sweeter, I didn't give up. After months of the painstaking tasks of sending in financial statements, applications, appraisals etc., the SBA finally approved the loan, but only up to the value of the nine aircraft that came with the flight school. I had to supply the difference, with a small note carried by the sellers.

From around November 2006 till July 2007, I was working extremely hard to get the loan to go through and work for all parties. It was a learning process with the Small Business Administration, but we made it work along with the SBA servicing company—the actual provider of the cash.

The SBA process isn't exactly what people think. To quote from their Web site,

"The SBA provides a number of financial assistance programs for small businesses that have been specifically designed to meet key financing needs, including debt financing, surety bonds and equity financing."

Guaranteed Loan Programs (Debt Financing)

SBA doesn't make direct loans to small businesses. Rather, SBA sets the guidelines for loans, which are then made by its partners (lenders, community development organizations and micro lending institutions). SBA guarantees that these loans will be repaid, thus eliminating some of the risk to the lending partners. So when a business applies for an SBA loan, it is actually applying for a commercial loan, structured according to SBA requirements with an SBA guaranty.

SBA-guaranteed loans may not be made to a small business if the borrower has access to other financing on reasonable terms.

SBA loan guaranty requirements and practices can change as the Government alters its fiscal policy and priorities to meet current economic conditions. Therefore, you can't rely on past policies when seeking assistance in today's market.

Venture Capital Program (Equity Financing)

SBA's Small Business Investment Company (SBIC) program is a public-private investment partnership through which SBA provides venture capital to small businesses. SBICs are privately owned and managed investment funds, licensed and regulated by the SBA. With the private capital they raise and with funds borrowed at favorable rates through SBA, SBICs provide financing in the form of debt or equity to small businesses.

SBICs are similar to venture capital, private equity and private debt funds in terms of how they operate and their ultimate objective to generate high returns for their investors. However, unlike those funds, SBICs limit their investments to qualified small business concerns as defined by SBA regulations.[3]

On August 1, 2007, I took over the operation of Modesto Flight Center. I spent much of the bureaucratic waiting time planning what I wanted to do: get certified as a Cessna pilot center, provide flight instruction, sell supplies, and do maintenance. I even redid the center's website—anything to get it to stand out from the pack.

As it turned out, we not only became a Cessna Pilot Center but MFC got an award from Cessna in August 2008 for doing an excellent job as a flight center. (See Appendix 1.)

The purchase process worked.

Modesto Flight Center Press Release
By Richard Corbett, Owner

July 22, 2007

Modesto Flight Center is proud to announce the transfer of ownership to Richard Corbett, who has begun a new chapter in the Center's twenty-six-year history. On July 22, 2007, Richard Corbett assumed ownership of Modesto Flight Center and has started the process to expand the center's current services. Soon he will add additional aircraft, additional maintenance services, aircraft sales, and aircraft waxing and detailing. Modesto Flight Center will truly be a one-stop shop for aviation services.

Modesto Flight Center was started over twenty-six years ago by partners Sandy and Dave Mesenhimer and Larry and Pat Askew. It was based on the premise of starting a flight school where customers would be treated like friends and family—a place to learn, chat, share friendships, and of course enjoy good food served every Saturday. Being passionate about flying, educating, and meeting new friends makes Modesto Flight Center stand out from the rest. And those values will continue with the new owner, Mr. Corbett.

Mr. Corbett's background shows that passion for flying and educating. He currently serves in the USAF Reserve as a pilot of KC-10 aircraft at Travis AFB, CA, and is a pilot for a major airline. He started his flying career in the Bay Area and went to college at San Jose State University. He is rated as a pilot and navigator in the US Air Force.

His current civilian ratings are an ATP and a CFI. He is typed in the DC-10, A320, B-737, BE400, and MU300.

We look forward to the future of Modesto Flight Center and continuing the passion, values, and vision the original founders instilled in the roots of this great organization. Please visit Modesto Flight Center online at www.modestoflightcenter.com or come join us on any Saturday at 11:00 a.m. for great food prepared by Sandy, and see for yourself that Modesto Flight Center is truly a place where everybody knows your name.

By the time I was interviewed for the article, I'd arranged agreements to provide the lab experience for two universities' online aviation degree programs. Computers definitely are valuable training tools in aviation. Ground simulators, in use since 1910, might even be considered an early form of online training. Students, however, need hands-on contact with real airplanes.

There was a lot to be done with the flight school. There were many administrative items to do, such as creating and introducing an employee handbook and establishing a "do's and don'ts" document to keep renter pilots and student pilots up to date on the rules of the flight school and standard aviation practices and rules. We had to upgrade the computer system with new equipment. We added an online scheduling system that tracked the daily flight schedule, maintenance records for the aircraft, and cost requirements of student pilots and renters.

In other words I tried to modernize the flight school to

bring it to a more computerized model of operation. This wasn't a big cost monetarily. There were some gripes from the customers and employees who were stuck in the more archaic structure. However, our advancements and upgrades were implemented and folks, when they saw the improved service, eventually adjusted.

At the time Modesto Airport seemed to welcome new management and a potentially revived and expanded flight school. Bill Latham, then acting general manager of Modesto Airport, said, according the *Modesto Bee* article, "Having a successful flight school is an integral part of being a full-service airport." He added, "It will bring additional capitalization, growth, new aircraft and additional instructors… I see [Corbett] revitalizing a great business and making it an even better part of the airport's program."[4]

However, Bill Latham was wrong, and I could only wish he had gotten the "acting" removed from his title and stayed on.

24

Chapter Two
The Fueling Farm Idea

Flight schools frequently provide fueling services for general aviation. The Modesto Airport, however, has had only one service since 1986: a company called Sky Trek.

In October 2007 I was approached by Rich Pinnell, a sales rep for Ascent Aviation Group. This company was the affiliate of Conoco Phillips, a major oil company. They inquired about my interest in adding a fuel farm to Modesto Flight Center. I was favorable toward the idea. I figured if we could pump our own fuel at our own costs, we could save thousands of dollars a month from not having to pay the high retail prices of Sky Trek. Additionally, we could earn revenues from other tenants on the field and provide fuel services for transient aircraft.

Interestingly enough there was a time when I did a lot of research on possibly investing in gas stations. In the past I interviewed multiple gas station owners to see how their stations were run, the investments needed, and if they were sound investments. Most people thought it was a good idea. But there were caveats to these businesses: be careful of what franchise you choose, and be sure to own the land so you have a say in the structure of the deals. Other than that, they mentioned that the markup in the convenience stores was excellent, but the fuel was miniscule. Volume is the key here, so I decided to pass on any gas station investments for the time being and moved on to other things.

Anyway, we discussed why it was necessary to have a second fueling service on the field. The airport pumped around one million gallons of fuel year after year. A lot of airports have a second facility on the airport grounds to promote competition and give consumers a choice. To use the flight center as an example, in the few months I'd been running it, fuel prices were my number one cost. Despite buying in bulk, I wasn't receiving a break from the only fuel service in the field—Sky Trek. They had been in the fuel business for many years with no competition to worry about. Therefore, they tended to have the highest prices in the area. Their prices were even higher than San Jose International Airport, which was not that far way.

Why had there not been a second FBO fuel farm at Modesto in the previous two decades, and why had no one else sought to establish such a facility? Readers may want to dismiss me as paranoid, feeling that people are out to get me. But to paraphrase an old saying, even paranoiacs have enemies. At least in my opinion—readers should make up their minds after reading this book—there is a reason why no fixed-base operators in the past eighteen years have been successful in placing an additional fuel farm at Modesto Airport. It is the clout and power that John Rogers and Sky Trek have, and the influence and effect that Mr. Rogers has had for a long time on the city of Modesto. (Mr. Rogers's neighborhood is far less of a happy place in Modesto than on TV!)

I've been approached by many people who have told me I have gone farther than any other FBO in obtaining a fuel farm at Modesto Airport. I've explained my position and the extensive hurdles I have had to endure from many people including other FBO owners, the FAA, multiple attorneys, consultants, the media, and pilots from various aviation communities. They all have said the same thing: "What you have gone through wasn't right. You have been done wrong, and this needs to be brought up to the right authorities so this doesn't happen to someone else."

As of July 2010, no efforts whatsoever were underway to establish a second FBO fuel farm at Modesto Airport.

I think a few words on fueling are useful. Typically, commercial airlines have contracts at large airports for their fuel needs. These are most likely set at certain pricing arranged between the companies. Sometimes, if the price of fuel at an airport is too high, the airliner may tanker fuel in order to continue on to its destination and not have to buy gas at an intermediate stop.

General aviation works the same way but is broader in terms of fuel servicing. You could have a full-service FBO fuel your aircraft for you, or you could go to a self-service pump similar to what you would do at a gas station for your car. If a general aviation field is pumping over a million gallons a year, you would normally notice multiple fuel companies around, keeping competition healthy. Some airports have multiple fueling services but do not even pump over one million gallons a year.

Modesto Airport had several attempts, to my knowledge, of businesses trying to establish a second fueling operation before my efforts. But those attempts failed; they never came to fruition. I was told these were all over a period of twenty years, and curiously I never got into any further discussions on how and why they were never successful in their fueling ventures. This was a tactical error on my part.

Interestingly enough, I was told by several customers of mine who had been around the airport for many years that my petition to sell fuel went farther than anyone else's had managed to go in the past.

Aviation fuel is transported and sold a lot like how standard gasoline is put in standard cars. The same rules and principles apply. Transportation costs may cause fuel costs to rise. The East Coast has a better developed pipeline system. At John F. Kennedy Airport in New York, for example, much of the fuel is pumped all the way from refineries in the Gulf Coast through a pipeline. Some of this pipeline runs under New York Harbor.

Competition also keeps costs down. Commercial airlines at a large airport have the clout to keep costs down even from a single supplier. JetBlue, Delta, or Air France could cancel a high portion of services to New York because fuel costs are too high.

General aviation customers are small, however, and do not have this power. They need a competitive market for airport fuel. Even if some pilots decide to patronize another airport, the loss of business would not be that great.

FAA Rules on Monopolies

Fuel services at Modesto Airport were run as a monopoly, with only one supplier. This wasn't fair but, under FAA rules, was allowed under certain limited circumstances. I didn't think that Modesto Airport met these requirements.

A monopoly at an airport that receives any federal funds violates FAA regulations and the federal law behind these regulations. The rule is described in an FAA advisory circular quote below,[5] which gives the principles behind which I applied for my fuel farm lease. The FAA works to ensure safety of the civilian aviation industry. It also works to make the industry work most effectively. Competition ensures the industry will be most effective.

1.1. **OBLIGATION AGAINST GRANTING EXCLUSIVE RIGHTS.** Most exclusive rights agreements violate the grant assurances contained in FAA grant agreements or similar obligations in surplus property conveyances. With few exceptions, an airport sponsor is prohibited from granting a right to a single operator for the provision of an aeronautical activity to the exclusion of others. See definition of exclusive right in Appendix 1. Accordingly, FAA policy prohibits the creation or continuance of exclusive rights agreements at obligated airports where the airport sponsor has received Federal airport development assistance for the airport's improvement or development. This prohibition applies regardless of how the exclusive right was created, whether by express agreement or the imposition of unreasonable minimum standards and/or requirements (inadvertent or otherwise).

1.2. **AGENCY POLICY.** The existence of an exclusive right to conduct any aeronautical activity at an airport limits the usefulness of the airport and deprives the public of the benefits that flow from competitive enterprise. The purpose of the exclusive rights provision as applied to civil aeronautics is to prevent monopolies and combinations in restraint of trade and to promote competition at federally-obligated airports. An exclusive rights violation occurs when the airport sponsor excludes others, either intentionally or unintentionally, from participating in an on-airport aeronautical activity. A prohibited exclusive right can be manifested by an express agreement, unreasonable minimum standards, or by any other means. Significant to understanding the exclusive rights policy is the recognition that it is the impact of the activity, and not necessarily the airport sponsor's intent, that constitutes an exclusive rights violation.

1.3. **EXCLUSIVE RIGHTS VIOLATIONS AND EXCEPTIONS TO THE GENERAL RULE:**
   1. **Restrictions Based on Safety and Efficiency.** An airport sponsor can deny a prospective aeronautical service provider the right to engage in an on-airport aeronautical activity for reasons of safety and efficiency. A denial based on safety must be based on evidence demonstrating that airport safety will be compromised if the applicant is allowed to engage in the proposed aeronautical activity. Airport sponsors should carefully scrutinize the safety reasons for denying an aeronautical service provider the opportunity to engage in an aeronautical activity if the denial has the possible effect of limiting competition.

   The FAA is the final authority in determining what, in fact, constitutes a compromise of safety. As such, an airport sponsor that is contemplating the denial of a proposed on-airport aeronautical activity is encouraged to contact the local Airports District Office (ADO) or the Regional Airports Office. Those offices will then seek assistance from FAA Flight Standards (FS) and Air Traffic (AT) to assess the reasonableness of the proposed action and whether unjust discrimination results from the proposed restrictions on aeronautical activities because of safety and efficiency.

As a practical matter, most airport sponsors recognize that aeronautical services are best provided by profit-motivated private enterprises. However, there may be situations that the airport sponsor believes would support the airport providing aeronautical services. Examples include situations where the revenue potential is insufficient to attract private enterprises and it is necessary for the airport sponsor to provide the aeronautical service, or situations where the revenue potential is so significant that the airport sponsor chooses to perform the aeronautical activity itself in order to become more financially self-sustaining.

An example of an airport sponsor choosing to provide an aeronautical service would be aircraft fueling. While the airport sponsor may exercise its proprietary exclusive to provide fueling services, aircraft owners may assert the right to obtain their own fuel and bring it onto the airport to service their own aircraft, but only with their own employees and equipment and in conformance with reasonable airport rules, regulations and standards.

2. **Single Activity.** The fact that a single business or enterprise may provide most or all of the on-airport aeronautical services isn't, in itself, evidence of an exclusive rights violation. What is an exclusive rights violation is the denial by the airport sponsor to afford other qualified parties an opportunity to be an on-airport aeronautical service provider. The airport sponsor may issue a competitive offering for all qualified parties to compete for the right to be an on-airport service provider. The airport sponsor isn't required to accept all qualified service providers without limitation.

The fact that only one qualified party pursued an opportunity in a competitive offering would not subject the airport sponsor to an exclusive rights violation. However, the airport sponsor can't as a matter of convenience choose to have only one FBO provide services at the airport, regardless of the circumstances at the airport.

The above material from the FAA relates in several respects to my situation. The FAA allows monopoly service only under limited circumstances. If Modesto Airport had been supplying the fuel service itself, this would be permitted. But this wasn't the case. The airport was allowing a private firm, Sky Trek, to supply the service.

The airport could deny my application on the grounds of safety, but my contention always was that there were no safety issues. This was backed up by the experience of the thirteen other similar facilities. This was also true if one included environmental safety.

As further backup and protection for the airport, had the application been allowed to go forward as it should have, the city and the airport would've had the chance to inspect and ensure that safety measures and environmental protection measures were in place before I was given the chance to operate. But they would've had to prove lack of safety, taking the burden of proof off my back.

The FAA doesn't require an airport to seek competition for a service. An airport authority can't be cited for unfair practice if no one else has applied to establish a service. But I had sought to open a competitive service.

There is nothing that says the airport or the FAA has to take into account the financial interest of the firms engaged in service. Competition has to be given a chance. Here the city thought Modesto Flight Center might initially take some business from Sky Trek but the net result would be an increase in total business at the airport. The FAA rules quoted above didn't require me to succeed. They only required I be given a fair chance.

FAA decisions can be appealed, but courts tend to support the rulings of an objective federal agency. Modesto Airport knew they had no grounds to deny my application under the above rule. But—and here is where they were clever—they never actually denied my application. By not actually denying my application—though they did eventually cancel the process, blaming it on my delay in paying for the environmental study—they didn't violate the letter of the FAA regulatory laws.

But it was my thought then, and it is my contention now, that they crassly violated their spirit. Appealing an unfair process, as I would learn, is always harder than appealing an unfair result. You have to prove harmful intent, which is harder than proving a harmful result.

This was in the future, though the near future. Back in August 2007, Rich Pinnell thought adding fueling services to the flight school would be a great opportunity. I agreed. After a few weeks of getting our ducks in a row, or so we thought, we set up a meeting with Jerome Thiele, the newly appointed airport manager introduced to the airport advisory committee on December 19, 2007 but on the job several weeks before that. Our initial meeting was at a local Mexican restaurant. We discussed the proposal. Thiele, new in his job and learning the political realities he would have to face, was all for it; he was excited to have such a project started on the field. He asked that I submit a formal letter regarding my request for the fuel farm.

In November 2007 I submitted a formal letter requesting a fuel farm lease. The intention was that the installation costs would be minimal because the tanks were above-ground and the majority of the project would be financed. In fact I had already been approved for a loan of over $300,000 for the installation of the fuel tanks. To the best of my knowledge, the tanks met common environmental standards.

Jerome Thiele informed me the process would consist

of getting approval of the airport advisory committee, then the economic development committee, and finally the city council. I was told the only function for the city council was to approve my new lease, and from there we could get construction started. But, as I explain in this book, the process to get this project done was mind blowing, to revive a phrase from the 1960s.

The exact instructions in his letter to me on December 11, 2007 are quoted below:

> Your request to install a fueling facility on the airfield at MOD must meet with the approval of the Federal Aviation Administration (FAA) before it can proceed to the city for review. Please complete the attached FAA form 7450-1 according to their specific instructions, and indicate on the enclosed map exactly where you intend to place the fuel tank. After you have completed the request, please send a copy to our office in the attached envelope, and forward the originals to the FAA as directed in the instructions. [FAA approval was obtained on May 1 of 2008.]
>
> While awaiting FAA approval, our office will work with you through the process for city approval, which we anticipate taking approximately 90 days from start to finish. Three sets of plans will be required for city planning and permitting review. The first steps will include review of the proposed plan by the City Attorney and the Risk Manager, as well as the Airport Advisory Committee. A new or revised lease agreement will be drafted, including

a provision for payment of a fuel flow tax to the airport.

Finally, the request will be presented for review and approval of the Economic Development Committee and then for final approval by the City Council. After a new City agreement is executed you will be able to proceed with the approved project. You will also need to obtain any necessary permits specific to the scope of the project before operations can begin.

Note carefully the last line of this letter: "You will also need to obtain any necessary permits specific to the scope of the project before operations can begin."

I wish, in retrospect, that I had asked for clarification. The wording of that one line, and its location at the end of the letter, can be interpreted to mean that permits had to be obtained before the fuel farm could start operating, after early state approval. There were distinct implications in the letter that no problems were expected. The text, for example, mentions that an agreement "will be drafted," "including a provision for a payment of a fuel flow tax to the airport." Why would I be told such a tax would have to be paid and that the agreement would include a provision for the tax unless approval was expected?

The December 2007 letter from Mr. Thiele, the airport manager, said he anticipated the process taking about ninety days. I read this as it might have taken ninety-three days, as most people, myself included, do not always remember to add a few days of safety margin. But 300-plus days was indeed far too long.

The December 2007 letter did allow them some leeway

for both time and conclusions. However, the general tone was virtually that of a form letter. One could logically assume all requirements would be mentioned, since the letter w written by someone who should have known the requirements and passed them all on. There weren't any sentences in the letter for the airport and city to cover themselves (*CYA* is the common term; I will leave it to the reader to guess what it stands for) along the lines of, "And any other requirements that might be seen as necessary as the project proceeds."

One couldn't read a rubber-stamp approval process in the letter, but it didn't hint at possible trouble. Most significantly the letter didn't mention a possible environmental study being required before the lease was approved.

The letter seemed to summarize the approval process. However, the city had no checklist and no plan for the steps in approving projects such as mine. In fact Jerome Thiele was quoted as saying to someone in his office that I was setting precedence on how to get a project going on the airport, and that the city really didn't have a formal checklist—it tended to decide off the cuff.

This would have been odd enough if at the end the project were successful. But delay after delay created by the city put me in a perilous financial situation. When there is no set process for doing something, it is hard to know what steps to take or to prove you took the steps. Should I console myself with the idea that the city was improvising delays?

The old saying tells us not to attribute to malevolence what can be explained by stupidity, but the end result was still the same. And too much of a definite and structured pattern arose for me to attribute these odd events to mere careless stupidity.

38

Chapter Three

The Real Process Begins

To cheat and jump ahead, there were blatant issues and discriminatory tactics that the city used throughout the process. The city seemed to want to hide behind the smoke screen of the required California Environmental Quality Assessment (CEQA), saying I hadn't sent the deposit check to start the process. But it all fell back to intentional delays: how long can Mr. Corbett go before we make him go away?

During this process and since, I was approached by other tenants on the field. I have been approached by the media and have been on the local news and the front page of the local newspaper. All these parties came to the same conclusion: I have been wronged in this process. The general conclusion is the City of Modesto, while saying it dealt with the process appropriately and the onus was on me to supply the cash to do the study, behind the scenes was ensuring my proposal was met by multiple hurdles throughout the way.

This was far harder than my buying the Modesto Flight Center to begin with. One might argue that they were different businesses, or that the MFC already existed. But I would raise the issue that the MFC didn't compete with the service Sky Trek was offering. One can speculate that if Sky Trek decided it wanted to offer a flight school, and I had not looked into a fueling service, they would've at least tried to find a way to come after the MFC. But this is speculative. I had enough to worry about with what actually happened.

When the whole fueling service process began, the airport manager was new in his job. He seemed enthusiastic at first but more and more political as time went on. He was learning the political ropes, it seemed—the way things were actually done in Modesto.

Just a note here: with all its political problems, I do not pretend Modesto is unique. What happened to me might well happen in another city. That is what makes this story worth reading and thinking about. That is also what makes it valuable to look into all aspects before opening a business. Look at the political realities as well as market and economic realities.

For those of you not familiar with Modesto, the city is located about ninety-two miles east of San Francisco and some sixty miles south of Sacramento, California's capital. In 2009 the city had a population of over 211,000. It is in the center of rich farmland; Gallo Wines is headquartered in Modesto, and agriculture is its main industry.

Director George Lucas grew up in Modesto. His first film, *American Graffiti*, was based on growing up there. However, the city council denied Lucas permission to film in town, so the movie was made elsewhere. They couldn't have anticipated the impact either the movie or Lucas would make. This showed a lack of foresight, a response to business pressures, or both, which foreshadowed the similar treatment of my own case.

Less desirable hometown boys include convicted wife murderer Scott Peterson and Congressman Gary Condon, who had an affair with a young intern, Chandra Levy, in his Washington, DC office. Levy was murdered. Condon was cleared of involvement in the case but lost his congressional seat. He was and is a jerk, but not a killer. I used to think these two men were unfortunate exceptions as found elsewhere in the country, but I sometimes wonder.

I do not know what reaction George Lucas received when he asked permission to film in Modesto, to make the city the place where one of the most famous and successful cultural franchises ever, *Star Wars*, was born. However, Modesto Finance Director Wayne Padilla, in an e-mail dated February 17, 2008 to Jerome Thiele, made light of my proposal and thought it would only make for a "spectator sport." The series of e-mails, including that catchy phrase, follows. I'm always glad to be entertaining, but there are other more serious aspects to this correspondence.

From: *Jerome Thiele*
Sent: *Wednesday, February 13, 2008 5:33 PM*
To: *Wayne Padilla*
Cc: *Fred Cavanah; Roland Stevens*
Subject: *Modesto Flight Center*

Greetings:

I was asked to visit with you regarding a proposal from MFC to enter into the aircraft fueling business. The new owner of MFC is seeking to purchase, lease, install and operate two 12,000 gallon above-ground fuel storage tanks, skid mounted with pump, filter and dispensing hardware, credit card readers for self-serve, and a 2,500 gallon jet fuel truck. This development will require aircraft apron pavement improvements (remove asphalt;

install buried electrical and concrete pads)

What requirements does the City require for: background checks, financial checks, performance bonds, business plan review, financial/sales forecasts, etc.? Are these requirements identified in the Municipal Code? MFC will be going through the standard City permitting process for this development.

Thanks,
Jerome Thiele

From: *Wayne Padilla*
Sent: *Thursday, February 14, 2008 1:25 PM*
To: *Jerome Thiele*
Subject: *Re: Modesto Flight Center*

Hi, Jerome,

There is no specific checklist for this kind of proposal. [Italics added by author.] However, there are several things to consider: does any other FBO have an agreement to provide fuel that specifies when/if/how another FBO would be allowed to offer fuel? I understand that with an airport fuel operation, one FBO borrows customers from another based on price and service so the total amount of the flowage tax collected by the airport will be unchanged. If you could forward the proposal to me, I can look it over and formulate some questions based on their proposal. That way, when we visit I can give you the additional information requirements that will be needed quickly.

                         Wayne Padilla
                         Finance Director

I think readers should note the part in the above e-mail about whether other FBOs have contracts forbidding competing companies from offering the same service. This clearly violates the FAA rules. I do not see obtaining a copy of the Sky Trek contract. But if such a clause existed, forbidding other companies from competing, it would be strong evidence against my proposal and would've been brought up in the process. It never was, leading me to believe the contract clause didn't exist. Anyway, I was never told my contract would not allow further competition.

Padilla to Thiele
February 17, 2008

Jerome—I've read the info that you sent to my office. From my perspective, whether MFC opens the fuel island or not will *only make fueling a spectator sport* [italics added], but for flowage fees, it is a zero sum game. Provided that they build a quality facility and it opens and eventually fails, the city can take it over and compete with Sky Trek if it wants to, or MFC can provide a guarantee (bond) that ensures they remove it if it fails. I wouldn't be too interested in their proforma, provided that these guarantees are in place.

> It looks/sounds like the two FBOs need to become friends and find a way to buy/sell fuel that allows each to be happy and profitable without the threat of competition from having competing fuel islands. I suspect that this may be what MFC is trying to accomplish with great bluster.

It is always nice to have one's motives doubted. And even if this were true, even if I wanted to effectively unite with Sky Trek, this still wasn't cause to deny my application. This would mean it violated regulations for Sky Trek to expand. I wanted my project to succeed. Also, was Padilla calling for illegal price fixing?

The part about having "guarantees in place" raised even further questions about why they asked for a financial statement. Padilla didn't seem to care if I failed, just whether there would be something left for the city. I suppose this was in keeping with the general principles of our free enterprise system, not to mention the FAA. What mattered wasn't whether I succeed or failed, just that I was given a fair opportunity and that I didn't do damage to the airport if I did fail. I could have lived with this.

Thiele to Padilla
February 18, 2008

> Thank you for the response, Sunday evening
> Sky Trek has pumped approximately one million gallons annually of Jet-A and 100LL aviation fuels for the past 23 years
> The Phillips 66 representative associated with

MFC projects that MOD Airport will see an additional 200,000 gallons of fuel sold annually due to increased marketing and promotion of 100LL piston aircraft fuel.

MOD Airport maintains a $06/gallon fuel flowage tax. That figure is scheduled to increase to $07/gal shortly.

MFC's initial focus was to get into the 100LL fuel business, but they recently added Jet-A.

Self-service fueling for 100LL is typical across the country. The credit card fuel stations (islands) are located on the secure airfield. The municipality/airport that I worked at prior to MOD operated a self-serve station with few headaches

I've completed surveys to see if Modesto Airport can support two fuel providers (it appears so.)

FYI—100LL is 100 octane (a typical car runs on 85-92 octane gasoline), aviation gasoline has a 4% lead additive (low lead), some race cars and four-wheelers use 100LL for increased power, Jet-A is a more pure version of Kerosene 100LL, has very flammable fumes, and Jet-A needs to be sprayed in order to ignite.

Padilla to Thiele
February 19, 2008

I understand that MFC wants the 100LL concession to fuel the R-22s and R-44s that they are acquiring. My strong suggestion is that they should be directed to prove that no better deal can be negotiated with Sky Trek before much more time is invested in the new proposal. With only $14,000 in flowage fees to be gained (possibly) from increased sales, I don't see this warranting much of a fight.

Read that second sentence again, slowly and carefully: "My strong suggestion is that they should be directed to prove that no better deal can be negotiated with Sky Trek before much more time is invested in the new proposal." Despite the fact that it still sounded like price fixing, I didn't see anything in the FAA regulations saying a service provider had to be able to provide services more cheaply.

It seemed very funny—hugely fishy, to use a stronger phrase—to have a sworn city official calling for two competing firms virtually to price fix and to have the city asking an applicant for a lease or license to prove the applicant can provide services to the city more cheaply than a competitor. The time for this is under competitive bidding for a contract. But there would not be any competitive bidding without competitors.

Chapter Four
Early Staff Work

Consideration of my proposal went on at least partly behind the scenes. All such processes involved behind-the-scene staff work—it is a fact of life. But there may have been another factor in play here. City staff work might be available under freedom of information laws, but this has to be requested. You have to know what to ask for. Board, commission, and city council meetings are open to the public.

I had onerous requirements set for me to accomplish throughout the process. I felt, and still feel, that the city was never organized and the items required were made up along the way. I felt I was being discriminated against. I took note of airport manager Jerome Thiele's words that my request was "starting precedence at Modesto Airport" in regards to the multiple hurdles I had to endure and items that needed to be accomplished.

On January 24, 2008, as discussed above, the airport manager received a letter from Michael L. Dworkin, lawyer for Sky Trek and a specialist in aviation industry business. He asked for certain documents from the airport: the Modesto Flight Center proposal; correspondence between MFC and the airport on the proposal; the minutes of all airport advisory committee meetings in which the proposal was discussed; the airport master plan; and the city and airport staff reports on the proposal.

It certainly looked like Sky Trek was gearing up for a fight. This was confirmed by an e-mail I received in early April 2008:

> **Richard Pinnell to Rick Corbett**
> *April 9, 2008*
>
> Just a heads up: had a good talk with Michael Dye this morning regarding the meeting he had with Jerry yesterday, then just had a call back from Jerry regarding my call yesterday about the noon meeting, while Jerry said his boss wanted to meet with just you—but it's ok to have me (and Bob) if you want. The meeting will be about what Jerry's boss thinks will be the cycle that your proposal will go through, that Sky Trek will try to delay (including suggesting that your proposal should be delayed until a min standards agreement is developed). Jerry and his boss I think just want to make sure that they don't get sued. All and all a positive situation in that they are taking your proposal very seriously (that's a good thing, I believe.)

Richard Pinnell was the regional marketing manager for Ascent Aviation Group. Unfortunately, he misjudged whether it was a good thing or not for my proposal to be taken seriously.

Two documents from this period show that things *seemed* to be proceeding in good order, if a bit slow and disorganized. The author of the first isn't known, but it looks like it was prepared by an airport official. Note that the environmental study issue is still not discussed.

Status of Modesto Flight Centers Proposal
March 20, 2008

Lease agreement: Working from the existing 54-page, February, 1989 Sky Trek Aviation Fuels, Inc. lease, a new lease agreement amendment, totaling 45-50 pages, is being assembled to support the MFC proposal. Once finished, the draft lease is subject to City Legal, Finance and Risk Management review. This lease is a major component of the MFC proposal advancing to the Council Economic Development Committee.

Rates and Charges: Linda Boston, Community Development, has provided the names of five real estate appraisers that the City has utilized in recent years. I have attempted contact with all five. One firm has provided a quote to complete the appraisal with final product available in six weeks after given the NTP. I will continue to obtain quotes from the other firms. A review appraisal may be prudent. This might be obtained from a CalTran Properties Specialist for minimal cost. Sky Trek has retained an Appraiser to support their legal case.

MFC Business Plan: March 12, 2008 letter to MFC requested this along with several other financial documents. MFC has retained a professional consulting firm that specializes in creation of Business Plans

Development: MFC has retained a well-known local contractor (Beard Ind. Park developer) to assist with the fuel farm facility development.

Helicopter Operations: MFC has secured one helicopter from the bankrupt Los Banos-based Silver State Flight instructors; mechanics and a roster of flight students are part of this new business venture. MFC has requested a lease amendment to secure additional office space in the fom1er airport administration building. This matter will be on the agenda for the April 14 Council EDC meeting.

The second document was prepared a few weeks later by the airport manager. Thiele had come back from the environmental review. The issue of the formal study had been raised but not yet settled. In a second meeting, it appeared that one point mentioned "city completes environmental study." A second point seemed to question the need for the CEQA, listing it as "CEQA?—this is a categorical exclusion."

This is interesting. In any story like mine, key elements of the evidence are not going to be available. This document looks like Thiele typed, or had someone else type, notes he made for his own use. I would like to have seen more explanation. But at least twice he suggested the city or lead agency was responsible for the environmental study. To most people this meant the city should have paid for the study. He also raised the issue of litigation and said this showed the need for "solid environmental documentation."

The document follows:

Minutes—Engineering Environmental Review
Modesto Flight Center Fuel Proposal
11:00 am, Tuesday, April 08, 2008

Meeting with the following City of Modesto officials at the airport conference room and fuel farm site tour: Ms. Vickey Dion, Senior Civil Engineer, Messrs. Patrick Kelly, Planning Division Manager, Brad Wall, Principle Planner and Dennis Turner, Acting Deputy Director—Operations—Public Works.

This covers a review of the proposal from MFC to pursue development of aviation fuel farm and events spanning from November 27, 2007 to present.

Discussion points:
CEQA—What is the project?

- Environmental review, Mass or R (?)—what environmental impact? Exemption from CEQA?—categorical exclusion
- Need definition of project, what is involved?
- City completes Environmental Assessment.
- Does lease agreement trigger CEQA review (Council Blue sheet?—check with City Attorney's Office)—Is this project ministerial?
- Is there a NEPA impact? Will this be triggered? Need for project description from proponent! Need to define process for proponent
- Plan review and relationship to zoning districts.
- Need working drawings, move through building permit process. Are we premature with EDC and Council?

- Are there previous airport environmental reports? Sky Trek—Should we ask for a letter with list of issues?
- Need solid environmental documentation with risk of litigation! Should city/airport hire own environmental consultant? [Does this allow for other options, such as the applicant hiring as well as paying for the consultant?] Typically head agency completes environmental studies.
- If project goes straight to building permit process, exempt from CEQA?

Need:
- Chronological order, establish timeline milestones.
- Who is responsible for what?

Site Visit Notes:
- Plans need to show: reconfiguration of ramp parking, paint striping and markings, storm drains.
- Need written description of development: drainage, utilities (sewer/storm/water/elec/gas/telcolhydrant), off-site information, what are public works requirements (fire hydrant near site).
- Bring in Steve Mitchell—review Article 30 requirements, commercial/industrial zone Brad - investigation of Article 30 application to proposed project.
- Need project description.

                              Jerome Thiele, Airport
                              Manager 75319

A strong indicator that this wasn't an organized process is that every senior city staff member who had to sign off on the process, including the city attorney, did so. The proposal would go forward for a vote by the Modesto city council.

At least this was what I thought.

54

Chapter Five
The Airport Advisory Committee

The initial airport advisory committee meeting, considering my proposal, was chaired by John Rogers, the owner of Sky Trek, a multimillionaire and philanthropist who contributed to the Modesto community for many years. He was very condescending, asked many questions regarding my proposal, and even asked for the potential number of gallons of fuel I would expect to see at the flight school. I didn't know at the time, and his response was: "Humor us. Just give us something." He should not have taken any part in the meeting.

My proposed fuel farm would have competed directly with Sky Trek. The airport manager and the other committee members were well aware this was a conflict of interest but allowed it to continue. In fact, when I asked the airport manager about it, stating this was an ethics violation, he said he knew about this and even mentioned the committee members had attended ethics training within the last year.

During the second airport advisory committee, John Rogers still acted as chair and made comments throughout the process. When my proposal was up for vote, he brought up that maybe "we should continue to look into this." But at that point, I made a comment that this was an ethics violation. It wasn't until then that the assistant city attorney, who was sitting next to him, remarked: "Yeah, John, you need to stay out of this." If it weren't for my interjection, the city would've allowed him to continue to join in discussions and make decisions at the meeting.

Two airport advisory committee (AAC) minutes are worth discussing in more detail. John Rogers, chairman of the committee, chaired the meeting. Keep in mind these are minutes—a summary written later, not a transcription of what was actually said.

Jerome Thiele was introduced as the new airport manager. As part of his report, he congratulated Sky Trek on its twenty-five-year anniversary.

Interestingly, and of some relation to my story, assistant city attorney Roland Stevens discussed AAC bylaws and meeting guidelines. He wanted to make procedures both more effective and more efficient.

Assistant City Attorney Roland Stevens Here to Discuss AAC By-Laws and Meeting Guidelines

Rolly discussed the guidelines for MC meetings based on provisions in the Brown Act (open meeting law) and answered questions about the committee's by-laws, which were officially approved by City Council motion in 1972. Rolly advised that the MC meetings are not to be held in closed-door sessions, and that all meetings need appropriate prior public notice.

The committee's by-laws can be amended, with City Council approval, if the group feels the scope of their duties or other by-law items need to be changed. The role of the committee is to provide advice and recommendations related to airport issues as stated in the by-laws, using the airport manager as a conduit to the City Manager and other appropriate city entities.

Members questioned how to streamline the city's process related to airport issues. The approval process of presentation to council committee and then City Council frequently takes several months, adding to delays and bogging down progress. It was suggested that a clearer mission statement or expanded authority for the airport manager might expedite decision-making and action.

After discussion, the group agreed to revisit this issue in six months, which will allow Jerome time to get familiar with airport issues and city functions, and to assess the situation. Jerome will report back to the AAC with his findings, and possibly with suggestions for changes the AAC might endorse to benefit airport function. Fred Cavanah stated that in his capacity as Acting Director of Transportation Services he will be available to assist Jerome in obtaining improved city response time and expediting progress through the necessary channels.

Jerome suggested that the group might benefit by having members attend a two-day course intended specifically to assist and inform airport board members, to be presented by AAAE next August in San Francisco.

Both the committee and the city had clearly not acted on these suggestions during my process. I'm not aware of any changes in this procedure in the months since.

At the next meeting my proposal for detailed discussion was brought up.

AIRPORT ADVISORY COMMITTEE MEETING MINUTES
January 16, 2008

Proposed Fuel Farm for Modesto Flight Center

Rick Corbett, new owner of Modesto Flight Center, Inc. (MFC), proposes installing and operating a complete self-serve 100LL Avgas and full service Jet-A refueling service at the Modesto City-County Airport. As proposed, two 12,000 above-ground tanks, a credit card reader and fueling equipment will be placed on a concrete tank pad (approx. 14' x 80'), located approx. 140 feet directly in front of the Modesto Flight Center offices (700 Tioga Ave.) on airport property.

This area is currently used by MFC for aircraft tie-downs. Signage would also be installed to direct clients to the refueling center. A 'Notice of Proposed Construction or Alteration' has been filed with the FAA. ConocoPhillips will be providing the fuel, and has developed a proforma for MFC. Rich Pinnell, the project coordinator, wasn't able to attend today's meeting. Based on the current Sky Trek fuel prices, Rick expects to save $2,000-$3,000 per month on fuel costs for MFC by having his own fuel operation.

Jerome Thiele has reviewed the federal grant assurances, City Code Title 7, Ch. 3 and 2007 California Fire Code related to this issue, and finds the proposal in compliance with all provisions. The City Fire Inspector has checked the site and has deemed it to be a safe location. This project is subject to environmental review. The City attorney has been consulted regarding a possible lease agreement.

Sky Trek Aviation currently serves as MOD's sole fueling source. Jim Van Heukelem and Todd Lambert were in attendance representing Sky Trek's interest in this issue. Their fuel tanks are located underground—a requirement at the time the existing fuel farm was developed in 1989. Their concern is that a *"level* playing field" be maintained, and that their long-term investment (fuel farm) at the airport isn't diminished by allowing another fuel service to enter with less up-front investment.

Jim reminded the group that the business generated by Sky Trek over the years has provided the airport with increased revenues. Jim stated that their fuel is competitively priced and he expressed concern that addition of another fuel source will create a situation where neither business succeeds.

Questions from MC members were discussed, including the following:

- What is the advantage to the airport of having

an additional fuel farm?
- What is the anticipated impact on current fueling services?
- What is the City policy/guideline for adding airport services?
- Does MFC qualify as an FBO?
- Does the airport have control over addition of business ventures by FBOs?
- What fuel flowage estimates have been projected for the new fuel farm?
- Does the airport have the right to deny this proposal?
- Does this create a situation where neither Sky Trek nor MFC will have enough business to be viable?
- How will the cost of aviation fuel be affected by the addition of another fuel business?
- What is the MC's role in this issue?
- What impact on other elements here at the airport will this project create?
- What if several other businesses propose similar services?
- Can current Sky Trek fuel flowage handle the increased business MFC expects related to their expanded Cessna relationship and increased aircraft traffic?
- What information is available from other airports related to the same issues?
- What's best for the airport?

It was suggested that a sub-committee be created

to evaluate the issue, in conjunction with MFC, Sky Trek and the airport manager, so that the MC can make a recommendation as this MFC proposal goes to the City for consideration. A motion was made (Adkison/Trevena, unan.) to create an ad hoc committee to research this issue, and to evaluate the advantages and disadvantages inherent in implementation of this project. Ron Jeske and Joe Trevena volunteered to serve as MC's representatives. Jim Van Heukelem and Rick Corbett will also be involved. Airport staff will coordinate scheduling as requested.

These descriptions of the meetings, accurate as far as they go, raise a number of questions. First of all, John Rogers is listed as not just attending the meeting but functioning as chairman and taking part in all discussions. He didn't excuse himself from discussion of the fuel farm. Bluntly, this is conflict of interest. Keep in mind that Rogers is the head of Sky Trek.

Modesto Flight Center would have saved $2,000 to $3,000 per month on its own fuel. The site plans presented no problems technically. Jerome Thiele stated the plan raised no issues with relevant federal grant programs or with the California fire code. The city fire inspector approved the site. "The project is subject to environmental review," read one line. The next line of the second paragraph indicated the city attorney had been consulted regarding a lease.

I suppose the environmental review line was the opening for the full-fledged report the city demanded. But the next line would have led a reasonable person to assume this referred to a final environmental signoff, when construction was done but before a final operating license was provided. This seemed to have been the view of the members of the commission, since no questions were raised on this issue.

The questions came about the impact of a new fuel facility on Sky Trek's business. Their representative raised the issue of protecting their investment. They demanded a level playing field, apparently meaning they were the only ones who got to play on the field. They found it an appropriate argument to claim the field wasn't level if I would be permitted to open a fuel facility that cost less than their initial expenditure. Underground facilities were the only ones allowed in 1989. Apparently, using new technology and operating under current regulations wasn't fair competition.

My response to this was generally along the lines of, "If Sky Trek loses business, tough. That's free enterprise." Equally, if my venture failed on a level playing field, that was tough. As for the competition, I thought MFC was likely to attract at least as many new customers as it took from Sky Trek. MFC would be increasing the size of the pie, not grabbing a bigger piece of it.

Most of the questions asked by the commission members focused on the economic effects of the proposed new fueling facility. Almost hidden were two questions about whether the AAC could advise on the issue and whether it could turn the proposal down. There was nothing in the FAA regulations saying rights for a second and competing service could be denied due to economic reasons or the convenience of the airport operating authority.

A second service could be denied if it provided a safety hazard. It could also be denied for reasons of efficiency, but the FAA went out of its way to say efficiency meant efficient use of airspace, and the FAA, as part of its traffic control, would determine this. The regulations stated efficiency "is not meant to be an interpretation that could be construed as protecting the 'efficient' operation of an existing aeronautical service provider for example."[6]

Causing economic problems for Sky Trek, therefore, according to FAA regulation, wasn't grounds for denying a second fuel service permission to operate. Other sources argued that my proposed fuel service would be as likely to increase total business at the airport as to take business from Sky Trek. But to put it bluntly, if I did take business from Sky Trek, that was tough!

It was suggested by John Rogers that a subcommittee be created to study the issue, and, needless to say, the motion passed.

Right before this meeting, an interesting document got passed around by Sky Trek officials. My copy came from papers supplied by Jerome Thiele. Even he didn't know who created the paper. It argued economic considerations for allowing competition, which did not appear in the FAA rules, however valid the economic considerations may have been for the economic viability of new and existing facilities. Even the paper said that though it was "highly beneficial" to conduct economic ROI and related studies, they were not required.

The paper also discussed minimum operating standards, ignoring that the FAA didn't require such standards but recommended them. Modesto Airport didn't have such standards when I applied for my fuel service. It still has not created such standards. They couldn't create them after the process started. Ex post facto laws are even banned in the Constitution, which, as far as I know, still trumps the Modesto city council.

How Many FBOs Are Enough?
Guidelines for Evaluating Airport Competition

Introduction
In the United States, competition is the very lifeblood of a healthy operation. Conventional thinking says a robust head-to-head rivalry is the best way to deliver the greatest value to airport users with lower fuel and service prices often heading the list of benefits. The Federal Aviation Administration (FAA) is on record as supporting hearty competition, to the point that some airport sponsors believe that compliance with airport minimum standards automatically signifies a deal no one can refuse. Just as an airport sponsor has the fiduciary responsibility to the airport's strategic financial security to consider all proposals, they also have the duty to ensure that giving the nod to a new business will not unduly harm the current or future airport environment.

There is no simple mathematical formula to determine the appropriate number of fixed based operations (FBOs) or specialized aviation service operations (SASOs) at an airport. Current guidelines used by airport sponsors during the competitive decision process consist of little more than anecdotes. But there are reasonable steps that can be taken to determine whether an airport sponsor should accept or deny a new business proposal or accept a portion of a proposal and whether these proposals should be formally solicited. This paper is designed to offer visionary thinking from aviation professionals that while certainly not regulatory in nature, can well serve as the comprehensive genesis of the thought processes necessary to more effectively promote and protect the economic health of any airport

Trying to understand whether competition at an airport represents an opportunity or a threat to existing businesses should start with a look at the airport environment itself.

The Airport Operating Environment

An FBO faces many of the same challenges found in any sort of retail operation. However, an airport service business differs from the typical retail store in at least two significant ways:

In the continental United States, it is common practice that retail operations do not actually own property on the airport. In fact, through commonplace reversion clauses, the facilities constructed on-airport actually revert to ownership by the airport sponsor at the expiration of the leasehold, and:

While a local auto repair store or restaurant, for example, might only interact with the local municipality or county government for the authority to operate, the petition to launch a new FBO requires a solid understanding of airport competition guidelines from the FAA as well as the local airport sponsor long before the first customer sets foot on the property. Advisory Circular 5190-5 essentially holds an airport sponsor accountable for ensuring that on-field competition is fair and open to all who have the resources to respond to an airport opportunity [such as by way of a Request for Proposal (RFP)] or who may see the airport as a possible growth opportunity for their business.

The FAA, in fact, specifically ties an airport's ability to garner Airport Improvement Program (AIP) funds to an airport sponsor's responsibility to maintain a level playing field, whereby interested parties can engage in commercial aeronautical activities by meeting reasonable requirements commonly referred to as minimum standards. Minimum standards mean just that, minimum standards established by the airport that any operator must meet in order to conduct business of a certain type on the field.

The type, level, and quality of products, services, and facilities offered can and often will exceed the minimum standards established by the airport. As the discussion about the application of minimum standards takes place, airport sponsors and service businesses are regularly confronted with challenging questions such as whether or not a single FBO already constitutes a violation of grant assurances, or whether the marketplace should decide how many FBOs an airport can successfully support, or even what the criteria could or should be for an airport sponsor to consider when rejecting an applicant.

Initial Analysis

Before an airport sponsor entertains or solicits proposals from prospective operators, it is incumbent upon the airport sponsor and the airport management team to provide existing and prospective operators with the "opportunity to be successful." This does not mean the airport sponsor has an obligation to "guarantee success"; it does, however, put the impetus on the airport sponsor to create an operating environment that is conducive to success, which, in turn, if successfully achieved, maximizes the benefits of the facility and level of services to the community.

This can be accomplished by ensuring that the airport has a current Airport Business Plan, a current Airport Master Plan (and Airport Layout Plan), current Primary Guiding Documents, and a current schedule of rates and charges—all of which must be uniformly applied and consistently enforced.

Key Attributes

Some key airport attributes to consider during a proposal evaluation include, but are not limited to:

Availability of land as depicted in the current Airport Layout Plan;

Existence of Primary Guiding Documents such as Lease/Rates and Charges Policy, Minimum Standards, Rules and Regulations, and Development Guidelines;

Airport Rates and Charges, including land

rents, improvement rents, commercial fees, landing fees, and fuel flowage fees;

Number of FBOs and SASOs;

Number and type of based aircraft;

General aviation fuel volumes; air carrier fuel volumes, aircraft operations;

A multitude of other local, regional, and national market and economic factors and trends.

A Regulatory Checklist

One of the most important elements to effectively evaluating a new FBO business proposal is a thorough understanding of regulatory measures including those promulgated by federal, state, and local government agencies having jurisdiction over the airport and its users. The federal government has had the language on the books about competitive airport issues since 1938. Most frequently quoted as it relates to the number of FBOs at an airport is FAA Airport Assurance 23.

In short, it states: "(The airport sponsor) will permit no exclusive right for the use of the airport by any person providing, or intending to provide, aeronautical services to the public." Despite the brevity of the statement, this assurance is frequently misinterpreted. Many airport sponsors believe they will violate the assurance if there is only one FBO at the airport.

The FAA's Airport Compliance Handbook, Order 5190.6/1., says: "Single activity on an airport does not necessarily translate into all exclusive right. The presence on an airport of only one enterprise engaged in any aeronautical activity will not be considered a violation of this policy if there is no understanding, commitment, express agreement, or apparent intent to exclude other reasonably qualified enterprises."

The agency clarifies its concerns by also stating, "In many instances, the volume of business may not be sufficient to attract more than one such enterprise. As long as the opportunity to engage in an aeronautical activity is available to those meeting reasonable qualification and standards relevant to such activity, the fact that only one enterprise takes advantage of the opportunity does not constitute the grant of an exclusive right."

Interestingly, some airport sponsors believe that once they have more than one FBO established, they can no longer be found in violation of Airport Assurance 23. That is also not true. FAA Advisory Circular 150/5190-5 defines Exclusive Rights: "A power, privilege, or other right excluding or debarring another from enjoying or exercising a like power, privilege, or right. An exclusive right can be conferred either by express agreement, by the imposition of unreasonable standards or requirements, or by any other means. Such a right conferred on one or more parties, but excluding others from enjoying or exercising a similar right or rights, would be an exclusive right."

This same FAA document outlines the purpose and the process for developing minimum standards as "the minimum requirements to be met as a condition for the right to conduct an aeronautical activity at an airport." According to the FAA, minimum standards must "promote safety in all airport activities, maintaining a higher quality of service for airport users, protecting airport users from unlicensed and unauthorized products and services, enhancing the availability of adequate services for all airport users, and promoting the orderly development of the airport." That said, it is not the role, per se, of the FAA to make a final decision about a new FBO on any airport.

One of the keys to maintaining compliance with Airport Assurance 23 is the development implementation, and consistent enforcement of the minimum standards. Minimum standards need to be objectively and uniformly applied to all FBO and SASOs. The FAA recommends [AC 150/5190-5] that minimum standards be tailored for a specific airport and not simply be a copy of another airport's document using a "fill in the blank" approach. While the FAA does not specifically approve minimum standards, the agency encourages airport operators to show them to their FAA regional office personnel for comment.

Airport Assurance 22, Economic Nondiscrimination, states: "(The airport sponsor) will make the airport available for public use on reasonable terms and without unjust discrimination to all types, kinds and classes of aeronautical activities, including commercial aeronautical activities offering services to the public at the airport." Further, it states: "The sponsor may establish reasonable, and not unjustly discriminatory, conditions to be met by all users of the airport as may be necessary for the safe and efficient operation of the airport."

The FAA is often quoted as saying, "Every FBO has the right to go broke." This does not imply that the airport sponsor must lease land and/or improvements to a company that will, based upon the sponsor's due diligence analysis, most likely be unsuccessful, as in being unable to fulfill the company's lease obligations. In addition, it does not mean that an airport sponsor must lease land and/or improvements to entities that seek to engage in activities that will have a detrimental impact on safe airport operations, even if the company is willing to meet the airport's minimum standards.

Some Basic Documentation
To ensure the provision related to uninterrupted quality of aviation products, services and facilities to airport users, the airport sponsor must also decide whether it should solicit new business proposals through an RFP process, or simply wait for companies to take notice and inquire on their own.

For airports focused on proactively developing new business opportunities, an RFP may be the most effective approach, since strategic results can be extremely difficult to project when an airport sponsor takes a wait-and-see attitude. [One caveat: The U.S. has a number of well-designed airports on the verge of economic failure because sponsors thought simply building the facility would be enough to entice tenants and in turn, customers.]

Demand/Capacity Analysis—A demand/capacity analysis identifies and quantifies the type, level, and quality of FBO or SASO products, services and facilities provided at an airport, comparing it to the level of "demand" being driven by existing customers and anticipated demand from future ones. The primary objective is to identify any service deficiencies on the field.

Return on Investment (ROI) and Internal Rate of Return (IRI) Analysis—An ROI analysis will determine the feasibility and/or viability of a prospective operator to add, or expand existing products, services, and/or facilities. This analysis can also be used to ascertain the financial impact or adding capacity to the existing airport operators. The first step in conducting an ROI/IRR analysis is to estimate the present capital investment, cash flows, and net profit of the existing operator(s). The next step is an estimate of the prospective operator's capital investment needed in order to deliver some minimal level of products and services that meet the airport's goals, while also addressing the deficiencies identified in the demand/capacity analysis.

Finally, the cash flow and net profit of the existing and prospective operator should be estimated by projecting the revenue stream for each operator based upon the level of demand that exists or can be reasonably anticipated in the future. Once existing forecasted investments, cash flows, and net profits are estimated for each operator predicated upon the underlying market share assumptions, the ROI and the more complex IRR analysis can be calculated.

Airport Financial Impact Analysis—It is critical for the import sponsor to fully quantify the impact of any expansion of products or services prior to soliciting new business proposals. Positive financial impacts may include increased rents and fees generated by the new operator; increased rents and fees generated by new based and/or transient aircraft owners/operators; and increased investment in leasehold improvements that may revert to the airport sponsor in the future. Negative financial impacts might require an improvement or enhancement of the airport infrastructure, increased maintenance or labor requirements of that infrastructure, decreased rents and fees from potential overcapacity issues as could be the case where operators pay a percentage of gross receipts or gross margin. In an overcapacity regime, the fees paid to the airport sponsor will typically decline.

Airport Business Marketing Plan—Although a well-designed airport business plan should clearly outline the goals of the facility, it is often not clear about precisely what action the airport sponsors should take in order to achieve their goals. Hence, there is a need for a marketing plan to develop and focus a distinct set of tactics necessary to achieve the airport objectives, whether they are financial or operational. Even a simple marketing plan should include strategic directions to issues and crisis management, community and media relations, advertising and trade show management, as well as specific financial objectives. A good marketing plan should also be sophisticated enough to segment customers by behavior, rather than demographics.

Working the Numbers

Regardless of whether a proposal is solicited or unsolicited, the evaluation process is the same. If the application was solicited, it is assumed that each of the three analyses and a marketing plan outlining a strategic direction for the airport has already been completed. If the proposal was not solicited, it would be highly beneficial for the airport sponsor to complete these items to gain a better understanding of the feasibility and/or viability of the proposal, as well as the potential impacts of a new business upon existing operators. While the discussion prior to selection or rejection or a proposal need not necessarily be long, it should be comprehensive.

A negative conclusion in itself may not appear as sufficient grounds to deny an unsolicited proposal. On the other hand, if the outcome of the Airport Financial Impact Analysis indicates that the proposal will have an adverse financial impact on the airport, there may indeed be reasonable grounds to deny a proposal.

Minimum standards that are current, reasonable, and appropriate for the airport are one of the most valuable tools that can be used to evaluate any proposal. The minimum requirements that should be identified in the document include, but are not limited to: qualifications and experience; scope of activity; land and improvements; facilities; certification; licensing; personnel; equipment; hours of activity; and insurance for each type of commercial aeronautical activity. If a proposal does not meet the airport's minimum requirements, the airport sponsor can readily reject the proposal.

To ensure the consistent delivery of quality products and services, it is highly recommended that any prospect be required to submit a business plan to the airport sponsor describing how it will develop, operate, manage, and market the new operation. An inability to develop a solid business plan should be an immediate red flag and possibly offer enough evidence to reject the proposal.

The airport sponsor has a fiduciary responsibility to establish and collect market-based rents and cost-based fees. It is imperative that the financial credibility of the prospective tenant be ascertained, potentially through an analysis of current and future capacity to acquire and/or develop the required and proposed improvements and facilities, and to acquire and/or lease the required or proposed vehicles and equipment. An in-depth study of the prospect's financial capacity through careful analysis of current financial statements, identification, and confirmation of available and committed funding sources is also critical.

Although deposits, bonds, and guarantees can be utilized to ensure that future lease obligations can be met, these items alone should not be the only basis for an airport sponsor's positive decision. The evaluation should be based on the ability of the new company to generate sufficient revenue to cover costs and expenses, sustain ongoing operations, and realize a reasonable return on investment. Besides financial considerations and obligations, the airport sponsor must evaluate the prospective tenant's capabilities as they relate to operational safety and levels of service.

Additional topics may well include (not in any particular order): an explanation of the relevant AC's portions of airport compliance handbook and airport assurance docs; an explanation of "opportunity to be successful"; a review of what it means to have only a single FBO on the airport; opinions of FBO managers giving us the "why" behind their views on multiple FBOs; a look at the positive aspects, as well as the potential drawbacks to multiple FBOs; an opinion on what agreeing to or turning down a new airport operator could mean to AlP funding; a guideline/checklist/decision tree for airport managers and sponsors; a "does anything here contradict NATA goals" question; an outline of competitive FBO issues in terms to which airport managers/sponsors can easily relate; and an explanation of the areas that can be misleading in this discussion—for example, "basing decisions only on fuel volumes."

Interestingly, I met virtually all of the requirements the memo suggested a new FBO should meet.

On February 18, 2008, I reported to Rich Pinnell a brief conversation with the airport manager. This might explain why the AAC approved my proposal.

Some other interesting information was communicated to me by Jerry Thiele, Modesto Airport's manager, on Friday, February 15. He stated he was surprised and disappointed that John Rogers was present at the first AAC meeting and even asked multiple questions regarding details and numbers. He agreed with me and stated that Mr. Rogers should have stepped down because it was unethical, and that every committee member must attend ethics training every three years. The last one they did was in 2006. All of those committee members should have made comments upfront but failed to do so.

The funny thing was (and by funny I mean strange) that the airport advisory commission actually eventually approved the proposal. John Rogers had been called on the conflict of interest and could no longer take part in the deliberations.

Follow-up to the Airport Advisory Committee Meetings

On March 24, 2008, I received a letter from Jerome Thiele, stating: "Enclosed are three sets of lease documents for your signature and corporate seal. Please return them all to me as soon as possible so that we can prepare them to go to the City for final approval early in April." The only mention of additional requirements was, "We also need to have current insurance certificates to present with the leases."

Everything was proceeding in good order. At least I thought it was, but it was not.

On the morning of April 9, 2008, I received a quick e-mail from my lawyer, Robert Hunt. He stated his interest in hearing about the political climate and asked if BP/Arco (yes, *that* BP) was willing to pay for a legal fight. This question would become an annoying side issue. Getting into the legal fight was the main issue. And this began with the political climate.

April 9, 2008, 7:04 p.m.
Rick Corbett to Robert Hunt

Just a heads up: Michael Dye, an aviation business consultant I hired to do my business plan, has had a meeting with Jerome Thiele (airport manager) today at Modesto Airport. Apparently, what Jerry told him is that Sky Trek is going to come at me and the city with full force to prevent my opportunity to offer fuel services. Also, there are a lot of other discussions that brought up many flags that Michael felt was absolutely asinine.

Michael has been around for many years, owns a Jet Center himself and can't believe what went on today with his conversations with Jerry Thiele. Jerry even mentioned to Michael that with what is going on and what is about to happen is the reason why there hasn't been another FBO on the field for the last 25 years. A statement that Michael couldn't believe came from an airport manager's mouth.

He is going to call you tomorrow morning to speak with you about what happened and what he feels is coming our way. I think it may be time to look into what is going on and I really do feel that I'm being torpedoed for trying to expand my business and muscled out. And everything I've witnessed, what Rich Pinnell witnessed, and what Michael has witnessed, shows that Sky Trek has done everything to try to stop this.

A side note: Jerry stated in the last two Airport Advisory Committee meetings that there is no Minimum Standards Agreement and that the policy that the airport has in place is the letter from the FAA. That letter states, in a few words, that not one business can have the exclusive right to provide aviation services to include fuel. This is the policy that the airport abides by, and it is an FAA document. He read that twice in both meetings so that everyone was in the know, including the owner of Sky Trek, who happens to be the chairman of the AAC committee.

Jerry has informed Michael that his boss wants to meet with me on Friday [April 11, 2008] to explain what's going on and the "political climate" that is involved. A sort of "facts of life discussion" as he put it.

Anyway, this is to keep you posted. There was an opportunity to offer fuel and I went for it. I felt that I could expand my business and I can't believe the actions that are taking place. I think this is the time I could use some help.

Lincoln Flight Center

We had aircraft parked in Modesto that didn't fly—and if planes don't fly, they don't earn revenue. So I did some research with the help of Cessna Pilot Centers, and we decided on Lincoln Airport, north of Sacramento, around March 2008. The airport didn't really have a reputable flight school on the field. Demographics matched what we were looking for—basically higher income earners and an older demographic.

We set up the facility in a small office attached to a hanger. We had some flight supplies and instructional material. We sent a couple of the aircraft and they ended up sitting just as much as if they were still in Modesto. For some reason, it didn't work out. We had logistical issues at times trying to get available instructors, but overall the students and renters weren't there like we had hoped.

As a Cessna Pilot Center, we tried to do open houses and barbeques to draw in people, but it was unsuccessful. It was disappointing because the intent was good, the demographics fit, and the business plan was there, but it didn't pan out like we had hoped. We closed that location in less than a year.

Legal Expenses

Financial help would not be coming from Ascent Aviation Group, a main investor in the school. Bob Hunt, my lawyer, had contacted them to see if they would help with legal expenses if I had to fight the city.

> *April 9, 2008, 5:02 p.m.*
> **Richard Pinnell to Rick Corbett**

We can talk more about this Friday, but without asking Ascent, here is my take on your (Bob's) request. While I'm surprised by the tone of the message "leave you hanging," I won't address that now. I also won't address the message from Bob other than to say that it would appear he is looking to see if there are deeper pockets that can be tapped should this become a legal battle.

I think you'd find that most fuel farm deals are completely set up by the ownership group of whatever business is going to be operating the fueling business. Most of us (contract fuel marketers) will on occasion offer to finance some part of the transaction, but for two reasons on this deal we decided to be more involved than normal. First of all, we are reestablishing the Phillips brand in California and are interested in doing whatever we can to achieve that goal; secondly, I wanted the experience of going through the process from start to finish.

That said—we are investing at least $225,000 in your business to help you get this part of Modesto Flight Center services up and running, but having a fueling operation will greatly increase the value of your business that Ascent Aviation Group will not enjoy. Yes, we get a great client; we'll hopefully sell you, over the years, a large amount of fuel and help you in other ways to grow MFC.

To ask us to fund (or even set up a legal team) seems to me to be asking too much investment in your business. If you feel we haven't been an effective partner to date, I'm sorry I thought (and have been told by my people) that we really have gone well beyond what's normal for the industry.

Hopefully, the information above has clarified my position, as you can see I have cc'd Dave on this message so he can be in the loop.

If you feel my response isn't in line with what you expect from your partner in this enhancement to MFC, please let me know and we can proceed from there.

Please address this email before I come down to Modesto on Friday for the meeting with you, Jerry and his boss, as it may not be beneficial to the outcome of the meeting if this situation is not resolved between us prior to the meeting.

When he responded the next morning, Robert Hunt seemed surprised by Rich Pinnell's response but urged me to stay calm and polite:

> Wow! Looks like I upset somebody by even asking the question. At the end of the day, if the City doesn't cooperate voluntarily in this process, the costs to fight them legally could be significant. And I know you don't have the money for that, Rick, and Rich is exactly right on that one—I'm looking for deeper pockets, and perhaps legal assistance that is accustomed to dealing with these issues.
>
> That said, it sounds like Rich's group doesn't get involved in these matters, so he doesn't have any legal help with that experience. I've dealt with

cities, counties and other public agencies for years on similar issues, but never on an FBO or even an airport or FAA issue. I have no doubt that I can handle it well, and that's what we'll do if Rich's group isn't prepared to help.

So go to the meeting, give them every opportunity to do what is right. Don't threaten, but let them know that you intend to do whatever is required to make this happen. Let them know that thus far you haven't had to call in your legal team, but they are standing by.

Not good, and it sounded a bit like Ascent was bailing out on me. But a few thoughts come to mind, starting with the fact that they weren't the ones causing me the problems. I'm not even sure how to suggest handling such a situation. It is always useful to have fallback positions, but I couldn't have anticipated the problems I encountered. Perhaps I should have anticipated political problems and tried to find a way to research Modesto politics. But what do you do then? Do you go to a potential lender or partner and ask if they will be willing to double their investment, effectively, if legal issues turn up?

The environmental issues began to arise more overtly in early May, a few weeks after the discussions mentioned above. On May 2, 2008, airport manager Jerome Thiele wrote me in response to some changes I'd suggested in the lease at the urging of Rich Pinnell. No direct mention was made of an environmental study being required. The letter did mention MFC would be responsible for environmental testing of the site. But this was mentioned in connection with due diligence. I interpreted this to mean I was responsible for ensuring the site was tested for environmental damage. MFC would also have to have a deposit to cover any ground cleanup from contamination.

This letter was another opportunity to raise the issue of a formal and expensive environmental study. This wasn't done.

The minutes of a May 12, 2008 meeting that Thiele attended along with Roland Stevens and Dennis Turned are quite interesting. The first line reads: "CEQA—another fuel farm, bad idea next to the existing site." Why was another fuel farm a bad idea? Where there possible environmental or economic problems for Sky Trek?

On May 15, 2008, Thiele wrote me about the possibility—not the probability—of the formal environmental study. He also mentioned they had not yet received the business and personal financial statements.

Why was it still only "quite possible" that the environmental study would be needed? Were they waiting for my financials to make up their mind?

Chapter Six
Environmental Issues

In much of the above, I use the term *environment* in probably its less common but equally correct use—the factors with which I had to deal and the context in which I had to work. But *environment*, in its common use of things dealing with nature, air, water, etc., became an issue in the whole story.

My contention is that it wasn't a real issue; the requirement of an expensive environmental study—the CEQA—was not an issue but a tool designed to stop my project in its tracks and maintain the monopoly at the Modesto Airport. In many ways, from their point of view, this was a good tool. Arguing against doing such a study put me in the position of arguing against environmental protection.

I was actually arguing against unfair procedures. Fair procedure is to ask someone to get their ducks in a row even if there are a lot of ducks. Unfair procedure is to encourage more ducks to fly in. Some things can be explained by coincidence. There is an old saying—never attribute to malevolence what can be explained by stupidity. But there is another saying: Fool me once, shame on you. Fool me twice, shame on me. Fool me more than that…

The whole theme of this book is that what happened was too much to explain away by something other than someone pulling strings to keep me from establishing my fuel facility. It isn't the comedy of errors I once thought it was. I wish it was, because errors can be corrected. There is too much cohesion in my story to be explained by anything other than a pattern. This may well be my opinion, but read on and weigh the evidence yourself. To paraphrase an old saying, when you hear quacking and see feathers and web footprints, you might conclude there are at least a few ducks in the area.

The whole idea of delay rather than out-and-out refusal fits with this pattern. Decisions, particularly negative ones, can be appealed. Appealing delay—even abnormal delay—is a far harder process.

Cost was an issue—perhaps the major issue—with the environmental study the city decided to require. Before the lease was approved, I would have to pay for the study. After the lease was approved, when environmental inspections would still be required, when safety would still have to be approved, the city and/or the airport would have to pay. Before the lease was approved, I would have to prove the proposed fueling facility was environmentally safe. Afterward, they would have to prove it was not safe. Their task was easier, as they could point to specific problems. I would, in effect, have to prove no problem would occur—and proving a negative is always iffy.

I would be given a chance to correct any problems that were found in the licensing inspection. This was uncertain if problems were identified before.

It is hard to argue against concern for the environment. But this isn't what I was doing. I was certainly prepared to take reasonable environmental and safety precautions. If nothing else, they are good business. And flying, by its nature, gives one a chance to see and appreciate the environment. So what about the safety of the technology I was planning to use in the fueling facility?

Environmental standards for above- and below-ground fuel tanks are strict, designed to prevent fuel leaks, to minimize standards from those that might occur, and to minimize potential damage from fire. Above-ground tanks have stricter standards for location in case of fire, to keep the fire from spreading. Dikes are generally required around the tanks to keep any leaks or spillage from spreading. Above-ground tanks have to sit on a base, usually cement, but also be raised from the base by secure and steady legs.

Tanks buried in the ground have their own standards along with similar protective shielding around the tanks. The ground itself, to some extent, offers safety protection. But there are major advantages to above-ground tanks. Underground tanks are more expensive to install and maintain. Funds saved on installation and maintenance can be fed back into a business and used for additional safety measures. Safety and environmental standards have improved over the years, but older facilities are usually grandfathered in, meaning they do not have to meet newer standards.

Gas vapor can leak from an underground tank. This can create a major hazard if not spotted early.

Perhaps primarily, all tank owners have a self-interest in keeping their equipment as safe and green as possible. Bad publicity, when this isn't the case, can prove just as financially damaging as any accident or even more so. But above-ground tanks are far easier to monitor. If the tank is above-ground, the best way to monitor it is probably just to take a look. Potential problems might be spotted visually even before they arise. They can be fixed. Even if fixing isn't legally required, it would be a good idea to do so.

No such easy monitoring is available for below-ground tanks. It would be difficult to spot problems below ground, aside from regular checks and when the problems become major. As far back as 1994, for example, in Humboldt County, California, they needed the emergency installation of an above-ground tank because of a continuing leak of uncertain starting time discovered in a below-ground tank. The emergency agenda item that approved the above-ground tank stated, "Inventory reconciliation (stick readings) indicating a continuing loss of fuel…" This high-tech method of checking fuel is the same stick used to check oil in a car.[7]

The issue arose so quickly, with such urgency, it had to be given an emergency place on the board's agenda after the formal agenda had been announced. Even if an above-ground tank had not been regularly inspected, someone would've seen a leak big enough to require replacing the whole tank. Repair would've been more feasible for the above-ground tank.

These realities account for why, of the thirteen local fuel farms already in place using the design I proposed, there had never been an environmental problem. There was no new technical information brought to light during the approval process. There was also no environmental emergency, in Modesto or elsewhere, that might have justified an additional environment-related requirement. Finally, lease approval wasn't the final environmental check on my project. Even if a formal environmental study were required, it should have come after the lease approval.

There is an interesting chronology that can be traced in letters from Sky Trek's lawyer to the city and airport authority.

January 24, 2008

Mr. Jerome Thiele, Airport Manager
Modesto City-County Airport 617 Airport Way
Modesto, CA 95354-3916
Re: Modesto Flight Center—Proposed Fuel Farm Development

Dear Mr. Thiele:

As a follow-up to our telephone conversation of earlier today, and my subsequent conversation with City Attorney Roland Stevens, this office represents Sky Trek Aviation.

It is my understanding that Modesto Flight Center has proposed construction of a new fueling facility.

I would appreciate your providing me with copies of the following:

1. Modesto Flight Center's proposal;
2. Correspondence between the Airport and Modesto Flight Center concerning its proposal;
3. Minutes of all Airport Advisory Ccm1Tlitter: meetings at which this proposal was discussed;
4. Airport Master Plan; and
5. City and Airport Staff Reports concerning this proposal.

I would also appreciate your providing this office with notification of all future public meetings concerning this proposal.

Should you wish to discuss this request, please do not hesitate to give me a call.

>With best regards,
>Very truly yours,
>Michael L. Dworkin

This letter was copied to city attorney Roland Stevens and to an official at Sky Trek Aviation, Jim Van Heukelem. A second letter, on February 5, 2008, was addressed to Jerome Thiele and, this time, to John Rogers in his position as chairman of the airport advisory committee.

>It is my understanding that Modesto Flight Center's proposed fueling facility project is scheduled for the discussion at the next meeting of the Airport Advisory Committee on February 20, 2008.
>
>My client has requested that I participate in these proceedings but I am scheduled to be out of town on February 20.
>
>Accordingly, this is to request that this matter be deferred until the March AAC meeting.
>
>I am still awaiting Mr. Thiele's response to my January 24, 2008 letter in which I requested copies of the following:
>
>1. Modesto Flight Center's proposal;
>2. Correspondence between the Airport and Modesto Flight Center…concerning its proposal;

3. Minutes of all Airport Advisory Committee meetings at which this proposal was discussed;
4. Airport Master Plan; and
5. City and Airport Staff Reports concerning this proposal.

I would also appreciate your providing this office with notification of all future public meetings concerning this proposal.

On February 7, 2008, according to the cover letter, the airport manager sent Sky Trek's lawyer the following documents:

1. Modesto Flight Center's proposal documentation
    a. FAA Form 7460-1 Notice of Proposed Construction
2. Documents provided to Modesto Flight Center
    - Title 7 - Public Works, Chapter 3 - Modesto City-County Airport
    - Chapter 11 Aviation Facilities - 2007 California Fire Code
    - *Note: Representatives of Modesto Flight Center were asked, and did, visit with the City of Modesto Community Development Center regarding permits, submission of plans, plan review and other requirements.*
3. "Draft" Minutes of the Wednesday, January 16, 2008 Regular Meeting of the Airport

Advisory Committee
  a. Handout from subsequent January 24; 2008 AAC Workshop
4. "Draft" 2002 Airport Master Plan Booklet (not approved or adopted by Modesto City Council) Red Binder
  a. Excerpts of the April 1993 Master Plan regarding fueling services
5. City and Airport Staff Reports concerning this proposal.

The February 13, 2008 letter included the following:

1. November 27, 2007 letter from Mr. Corbett regarding his request for fuel service authorization for Modesto Flight Center, Inc.
   - Airport Advisory Committee Meeting Minutes, as approved but not signed, for January 16, 2008
   - "Draft" Minutes of Wednesday, February 20, 2008 Regular Meeting of the Airport Advisory Committee
   - Agenda for Wednesday, March 19, 2008 Regular Meeting of the Airport Advisory Committee
   - Weekly Reports from Airport Manager to Public Works Director dated February 12 through March 12, 2008
2. City of Modesto "100 Year Flood Zone" map as found in FEMA website
3. Copy of the Draft 2002 Airport Master Plan,

not adopted by the City Council

I didn't even realize it at the time, but Thiele sent more to Dworkin than the lawyer requested. This was not required, particularly since the letter wasn't a formal subpoena, nor did it include a phrase along the lines of "and anything else relevant to this issue." Interestingly, the question of the environmental study appeared in Dworkin's letter of March 3, 2008 to the airport manager.

It is curious that the material seems not to have gotten to Dworkin. The letter commented on not getting some documents but also seemed to refer to specific information about the project. This is one mystery of the story. Perhaps Dworkin had another source for his information—he read or knew about the documents but didn't get formal copies. Rogers, as chairman of the airport commission, would've had access to all documents I filed. I think it likely—though this is one of the things I can't prove—that he would've communicated the information in the documents, if not actual copies, to the lawyer for Sky Trek—his lawyer.

As to why Dworkin was asking for documents I think he had already read, perhaps he was laying the groundwork for possible legal action, which included his complaint about procedure not being followed. He also might have needed actual documents or certified copies of any legal action. By my complaint isn't with Sky Trek's lawyer, at least not overall. He was doing what he got paid to do.

In his letter dated March 3, 2008, Dworkin complained about not getting the documents he requested. He also complained about his request to delay discussing the matter until he could attend the meeting. He complained that "with all due respect, this is patently unfair."

The letter then gets interesting. Aside from this procedural irregularity, Sky Trek opposed this proposal on the following substantive grounds:

1. The Airport has not promulgated any minimum standards;
2. There is some question as to whether the project is consistent with any current Master Plan, if even such plan should exist;
3. Modesto Flight Center has yet to provide a viable business plan;
4. Modesto Flight Center has yet to provide evidence of liability insurance covering risks attendant with this project;
5. The installation of "skid" tanks creates certain inherent safety issues, which the Airport has not addressed;
6. The location of Modesto Flight Center's proposed fuel farm places it at an unfair competitive advantage to Sky Trek's existing fueling facility; and
7. There is no evidence that the Airport has taken the requisite environmental reviews and studies.

These objections are not necessarily all-inclusive. Our investigation is continuing and upon our review of the documents that we have previously requested, there may be additional grounds for objection and opposition to the project.

> For the third time, we request that you providing this office with notification of all future public meetings concerning this proposal.

Again, how did he know these things if the documents he requested didn't arrive? Anyway, for that matter, why did they not arrive? And if they didn't arrive, why not call the airport to ask? The lawyer always had the option of sending someone, or going himself, from San Francisco to Modesto. This is about a two-hour drive each way, but Sky Trek could be billed for the time and travel expenses.

By the middle of the year, the issue should have been settled.

On May 8, 2008, the FAA approved my proposed fuel service operation. On May 22, 2008, the Modesto public works director wrote the economic development committee, urging what basically amounted to acceptance of my proposal.

Reasons for Recommendation

Here are some relevant paragraphs:

> Direct staff to proceed with negotiations with Modesto Flight Center...for land use at the Modesto Airport and return to the City Council with a lease agreement for review and approval.
>
> MFC, Inc. wants to expand its business and proposes to lease airport property for the operation of a fuel facility, providing fuel to local pilots and others who fly into Modesto City-County

Airport. The airport manager and the Airport Advisory Committee approve of the concept on the basis of providing fuel services that are conveniently located and competitively priced for aircraft operators who utilize the Modesto Airport. Staff expects that a mutually acceptable lease agreement can be negotiated that will address the future maintenance, operation and retention of the new fuel facility.

Revenues from this venture will help the Modesto City-County Airport continue to be self-supporting. Airport property leases generate revenue for airport operations, as do fuel sales.

Finally, on June 22, 2008, the City of Modesto Community Development Department issued a finding that my project was "statutorily exempt" from the CEQA study requirements.

That should have been that. However, it was not!

One week later, on June 30, 2008, thinking ahead, I contacted Michael Dye, an aviation business consultant. He began to look in to selling the business or bringing in a partner to help further the fuel farm process. I felt, at this point, that I needed to start some sort of exit strategy or bring in someone who had deeper pockets and could get this fuel farm completed.

Over the next couple of months, Michael had interested parties, but none really came to fruition. We started to get worried about the mounting debt and increasing fuel prices, so we had to do something desperate before things became dire.

Chapter Seven

Hey, Gang! Let's Do an Environmental Study!

The first tipping point in this project, the first potential roadblock, was a January 24, 2008 letter from Sky Trek's attorney. It didn't directly or indirectly raise environmental issues.

The February 5 follow-up letter, asking that the meeting of the airport board be postponed, also didn't mention environmental studies. Interestingly, it reminded Thiele that he had not responded to the January 24, 2008 letter. The second letter was co-addressed to John Rogers. Thiele finally responded on February 13, 2008.

I'd met or was meeting all of the requirements for which, as of December 2007, the related information existed. The city council had to approve the basic idea of the facility. But they apparently had the legal right—or thought they had— to add conditions to a personal plan, and they did so. They could also effectively ensure the conditions would not be possible to meet, though this certainly can't be legal.

An e-mail I received on February 15, 2008 from Robert Hunt indicated that agenda item materials had to be made available to the public. Was this the ostensive reason to release/leak my personal financial statements?

At least some city staff did like my proposal.

To quote the salient parts of this document:

First, we can expect that the new operation will draw between 10 and 15% of the volume of the current operator, will that affect their bottom line, of course. But where does it say that any operator is guaranteed a certain return when they go into business. In fact, the current operator has had many years of a situation that in reality can never be expect in any business venture. It has been mentioned that the current operator has paid the Airport millions of dollars over the years in fees from the pumpage of fuel; in reality it has been the FBO customers that have paid those flowage fees, not the FBO—those fees would've been paid regardless of who sold the fuel

What it will do, and what should have been happening all along, it will cause both operators to push their vendors (suppliers) to offer the best deals possible; long-term this should have a positive effect on the overall GA community at the Modesto Airport.

Now, it would not make any sense at all to make the investment required to start a fueling operation if all you were interested in was a part of the current gallonage being pumped. The Modesto Flight Center (as Sky Trek [sic] sure does) plans on marketing their fueling operation to local and transient aircraft, but because they are being supplied by a different vendor (and have a different core business model) their marketing will be directed towards its vendor's client base and not the base that is supported by the Sky Trek vendors client base.

Additionally, Ascent and Phillips offers advertising to its clients based on sold fuel; however, in the case of Ascent we will front some of those dollars to jumps start a new operation. Phillips also offers the Websmart program to further enhance its clients advertising and marketing efforts. This will benefit the Modesto Airport in several different areas. First of all, the Modesto Flight Center will be marketing to a new group of GA clients that I'm sure has never been courted by Sky Track. Secondly, I'm sure that the current operator will expend marketing dollars in an attempt to increase market share and gallonage, and both of those efforts will increase GA traffic at Modesto.

Also, the airport manager indicated that he has plans to attract another commercial carrier to the airport that might offer service to the east. Perhaps having a second fueling service on the airport will help in negotiation, whatever services the potential airline might need I'm sure they would be pleased that two operators to bid on those needs as opposed to being forced to negotiate with a single FBO. In fact I think it would be a reasonable assumption might be that an airport with a single FBO might weigh against a favorable decision.

I understand that someone raised the question early on: 'Why do we need a new fueling operator?' I would suggest that the very fact that someone asked the question is why a new operator is needed. New competition will cause new market efforts to build business at the airport, which will increase flowage fees to the airport, better support the GIA community in and around the Modesto area, keep more of the fueling dollars at Modesto, etc.

Interesting ideas in that memo. The airport management should have welcomed a second fueling facility, not merely obeyed the law and allowed it to start, as it would have helped to increase the size of business at Modesto Airport. All sides probably would have gained, according to this memo.

Looking over letters from Jerome Thiele, it looked like the environmental study was mentioned before they received the personal financial statement. But the exact words in the letter were "it is quite possible" that such a study would be needed. In some ways, on the surface, this could have been standard boilerplate. And I guess for any construction project it was "quite possible" that such a study would be needed. But I didn't see anything in the documents as to why they suddenly decided this study was needed.

Environmental impact is a big thing to forget. The study wasn't mentioned in the first letter to Thiele, and he didn't mention it when we first met to discuss the project.

The fact is that every senior city staff member, including the attorney, signed off on the proposal for my fuel farm and then they all approved it to go forward for vote by the city council. In that agenda, the statement of exemption was included, and it wasn't included until the letter from the attorney for Sky Trek stated CEQA was required. The assistant city attorney, Roland Stevens, pulled it without informing me or my attorneys at the time. And in an internal e-mail, the city wanted me to pay for the entire CEQA, stating the city would control it; this was to avoid a lawsuit from Sky Trek.

The city insisted they would get this rectified quickly, but the delays continued to mount. Dennis Turner promised an appraisal for my lease by July; I never received it. There was little to no communication for over a month after it was pulled from the July city council meeting. It wasn't until around September that the city mentioned various costs for a CEQA to be done. Jerome Thiele at one point mentioned to me that I could obtain my own CEQA person. But later in the day he called me back and stated the city would do the inspection and have full control.

I was pulled from the July 8, 2008 city council meeting. It wasn't until September 8, 2008 that the city finally officially notified me a CEQA was required and they had an estimate for a consultant. That letter contained a timeline of five weeks to complete. But the timeline Susana Wood, the city attorney, presented to us in November showed over six months. Why such a large discrepancy between the studies?

On July 22, 2008, Roland Stevens, the assistant city attorney, mentioned in an internal e-mail to Jerome Thiele that he wanted to ensure full control of the CEQA study. His main issue was to avoid at all costs a lawsuit from Sky Trek and incurring defense costs.

As he stated in his e-mail, "The deal should be that we do the environmental work and Corbett pays us for our costs." That had been the main issue from the moment Sky Trek got involved with my proposal. The city was so concerned about a lawsuit from Sky Trek that they would place delays at my expense to appease them. The contradiction in this is that when my attorneys, Charley and Gerry Brunn, mentioned they may sue the city, Susana Wood's response to was: "We have immunity. You can't sue us." So why did Roland Stevens fear a lawsuit from Sky Trek, knowing that the city (according to Susana) stated the city was immune? Was the city only immune from a lawsuit from me?

I'm not disagreeing with the fact that there may have been an environmental requirement that needed to be looked into. I certainly am not coming out against environmental protection. But environmental inspection occurs during the permitting process, after a lease has been approved by the city council. The issue only came up when Sky Trek's attorneys sent a letter on June 30, 2008 directly to the city regarding CEQA, days prior to my city council vote.

First of all, the city never brought up CEQA throughout the first eight months of this process. From November 2007 to July 2008, CEQA was never an issue with the city. The only time it was mentioned to me was in Jerome Thiele's office in May 2008. He told me, "Come outside, because I need to tell you something."

As we stood outside the airport terminal, he told me: "Sky Trek is going to bring up CEQA. Do you know what that is? It's the law of delay." Jerome Thiele insisted the city wasn't going to bring it up because, he felt, the planning department would have an exemption for the proposal. In fact, Brad Wall, the city's lead agency contact and principal planner, signed a statement of exemption on June 23, 2008.

Correspondence on the matter follows:

>-----Forwarded Message-----
>**From: Rick Corbett** *xxxxxxx@xxxxxxxx.net*
>Sent: *Jul 5, 2008 10:27 PM*
>**To: Charles Brunn** *<xxxxx@xxxxx-xxxxx>,*
>*xxxxx@xxxxx-xxxxx.com*

Subject: RE: Status on MFC

Charlie/Jerry:

No, it doesn't. Someone isn't telling us the truth. And I think this email from
Brad Wall, stating that the preliminary CEQA exemption statement was already prepared and was to be delivered to Dennis Turner, speaks volumes.

This is becoming very interesting, and I can't wait to hear what Turner, Wall, et al has to say about this.

Rick

-----Original Message-----
From: Charles Brunn <xxxxxx@xxxxx-xxxxx.com>
Sent: Jul 5, 2008 3:41 PM
To: Rick Corbett xxxxxxxx@xxxxxxxxxx.net
Subject: RE: Status on MFC

Rick:

To make myself perfectly clear, this does not meet the smell test.

Charlie
Charles K. Brunn
Law Offices of Brunn & Flynn

Email: xxxxx@xxxxx-xxxxx.com
Website: www.brunnandflynnlaw.com

By the time I got to the message, I would've already read the text of the e-mail. Besides, one of the best ways to get people to read things is to say "don't read this." But most people who get such messages by accident are not going to be interested in acting on the contents. During this story, the public release of my personal financial statements was my own experience with (intentionally) misplaced documents misread by other than the intended recipients.

But let's go back to the story:

-----Original Message-----
From: *xxxxxxx@xxxxxxxx.net* [*mailto:xxxxxxx@xxxxxxxx.net*]
Sent: Saturday, July 05, 2008 12:24 PM
To: Charles Brunn; Gerald Brunn
Cc: michael@xxxxxxxxx.com
Subject: FW: Status on MFC

Jerry/Charlie:

Below is the email traffic between Brad Wall and Rich Pinnell, and it looks like that document was prepared and ready to go. It looks like Dennis may have had it. This is becoming more questionable. It looks like that form was complete. And look at the date of the email, it states 6/18/2008. He had it

prepared in time.
   Please advise.

                    Thanks,
                    Rick

-----Forwarded Message-----
From: Richard Pinnell <xxxxxxxx@xxxxxxx.com>
Sent: Jul 5, 2008 9:28 AM
To: Modesto Flight Center <xxxxxxx@xxxxxxxx.net>
Subject: FW: Status on MFC

Good morning Brad,

Just wanted to check to make sure you had all of the information you needed to provide a complete OK on the MFC fuel farm project
                    Rich Pinnell
                    Regional Marketing
                    Manager
                    Ascent Aviation Group

-----Original Message-----
From: Brad Wall [mailto:xxxxx@xxxxxxxxxx.com]
Sent: Wed 6/18/2008 1:27 PM

To: Richard Pinnell; Modesto Flight Center
Cc: Dennis Turner; Jerome Thiele; Patrick Kelly
Subject: RE: Status on MFC

Yes. We have a draft Statement of Exemption (SOE) prepared to meet the CEQA documentation requirement. Once Dennis has a City Council date identified, and a draft Council packet prepared, we can add the SOE to it.

    I will complete the SOE document and forward it to Dennis this week, so that it will be available when the time comes.

                  Brad Wall, AICP
                  Principal Planner
                  City of Modesto
                  Community &
                  Economic Development Dept.

-----Original Message-----
From: Richard Pinnell [mailto:xxxxxxxx@xxxxxxx.com]
Sent: Wednesday, June 18, 2008 10:19 AM
To: Brad Wall; Modesto Flight Center
Subject: Status on MFC

Good morning Brad,

Just wanted to check to make sure you had all of

the information you needed to provide a complete
OK on the MFC fuel farm project
 Rich Pinnell
 Regional Marketing
 Manager
 Ascent Aviation Group

The statement of exemption was supposed to be filed with the Office of Planning and Research in Sacramento, California, but never was. The manager of that office, Scott Morgan, reviewed the document after I called and faxed him a copy, and he stated this document was legitimate and he felt my particular proposal of an above-ground fuel tank installation was exempt.

He wasn't happy that the City of Modesto may have violated the Permit Streamlining Act. He felt many other airports in California had installed above-ground tanks without CEQA studies. He further went on to state he felt the city couldn't pull something off the agenda from a city council vote based on just a CEQA study requirement.

This was especially since all city staff, including the environmental specialist, the director of planning, and the city attorney signed off on the proposal to go forward to the city council for the vote. Morgan felt there was "something not right about their process in doing that." He further stated: "The proper procedure is to allow the process to go through the city council for the lease vote, then off to the permitting process to see if any environmental is necessary."

This has been my issue all along. The city of Modesto doesn't know the process under which this proposal was supposed to go along because there never was a process. There were never established checklists or guidelines for me to follow. There were never any timelines in the beginning stages. Everything was done off the cuff from the time the approval process started and still had a chance through the decision or gradual evolution from objectivity to trying to wear me down.

In fact, an e-mail between Jerome Thiele and the finance director, Wayne Padilla, dated February 14, 2008, and Wayne mentioned "there is no specific checklist for this kind of proposal." It was so apparent, especially when the competition (Sky Trek) realized this proposal was a reality and got their attorneys and consultants involved. In the letter dated May 15, 2008 from Jerome Thiele, there was a litany of onerous requirements they wanted.

One of the items listed was that the city wanted to know about the financial outlook and any business plan for the helicopter operation. This was irrelevant to the fuel farm proposal. Also listed was a one-year audited, consolidated financial statement. I contacted my CPA, Joe Mendez from the Kemper Group, and he mentioned it was ludicrous to include that for a proposal like mine. He went on to say: "There is really only one reason why they want you to do this: they don't want you to have it. This costs over $30,000 to do and is absolutely not necessary." Mendez called finance director Wayne Padilla and said we weren't doing it.

I approached Jerome Thiele about these onerous requirements and he told me he was receiving a lot of pressure from Sky Trek and "it is what it is."

I said to Jerome, "I feel like I'm being discriminated against with all these requirements and delays. Are you telling me if any tenant on this field wants to do an improvement they have to do the same requirements you're setting forth with me? They have to go through the same process?"

Jerome Thiele's response was, "Sorry, Rick, that's just how it is right now. I can't comment further."

On June 23, 2008, about a week and a half before I went to the city council for my lease vote, Jerome Thiele sent me an e-mail regarding moving my fuel farm location near Sky Trek's existing fuel farm. I responded to the e-mail with multiple reasons why we weren't in agreement with that. On June 30, Sky Trek's attorney sent a letter via FedEx, vehemently asking for my proposal not to continue and bringing up CEQA. This was exactly what Jerome Thiele had mentioned to me back in May, although it was Sky Trek that was concerned about CEQA, not the city.

The city signed a statement of exemption.

Chapter Eight
Personal Financial Statement

In a way the sequence of events here is backward. The alleged requirement of an environmental study only arose after the city demanded and received a personal financial statement from me.

On March 14, 2008, airport manager Jerome Thiele sent me a letter requesting certain documents. The letter follows in full:

> Dear Mr. Corbett:
>
> The Modesto City-County Airport would like to request additional information from your business organization. This request comes after conferring with officials from Finance, City Attorney and Public Works Departments with the City of Modesto.
>
>   I. Five-year Financial Outlook and Business Plan—a Review of old vs. new operation
>   A. Include new aviation fuel venture and helicopter operation
>   1. One-year audited consolidated Financial Statement

      2. Personal Financial Statement based on generally accepted accounting principles
      3. Aviation Fuel Venture - Fuel Farm Development and Truck Operation
  B. Construction Budget
Identify dollars and time to accomplish task (construction cost estimated by design architect or contractor)
II. Confirmation of construction financing or other source of construction monies
  A. Performance Bond Commitment and Type (to complete project)
  B. Proposed terms of an agreement with the City regarding potential for fuel farm to cease operation and either be removed at your expense or assigned to City.

The Airport Office is assembling a lease to support the aviation fuel operation that will detail financial, reporting, insurance, fire safety and FAA Airport Certification requirements. We would appreciate obtaining the above requested documents within thirty days. Contact me directly with any questions.

                        Sincerely,
                        Jerome Thiele
                        Airport Manager

In addition to a business financial plan and information on

what I would do if the project shut down—reasonable requirements on their face—another requirement mentioned in that letter was a personal financial statement. Including this in proposal materials made the statement public. Going along with the process, I included it.

Since then I've had several attorneys, consultants, and others state there are issues with including the personal financial statement. The consultant who did my business plan and proposals included my personal financial statement in the business plan. But he also stated there was a confidentiality request not to allow others to view it, and the intention was for this proposal only.

We believe that wasn't the case. We feel there may have been a breach in that confidentiality.

This is one of my biggest questions. Why did they need the personal financial statement? Why weren't they satisfied with documented assurances of financing for various phases of the process? Any involved lenders and equipment suppliers would've already checked my finances. If the city really needed to know something about my personal finances, why not ask for a standard credit check?

Perhaps because a credit check only tells about my past credit record and how well I've paid my bills in the past. My credit rating would the same whether I was broke but paid all due bills on time or had massive amounts of cash available. Someone planning a delay campaign would want to know the depth of my pockets.

I can understand their wanting to do a credit check, to get an idea of my basic reliability as the owner of the proposed fueling facility. I can even understand it despite Modesto Finance Director Wayne Padilla's e-mail stating that all they really needed was a guarantee that if the business failed, I would either remove the facilities or turn them over to the city. I can understand a business plan with financing spelled out, and this was requested and provided.

But a regular credit check, it can't be emphasized too often, only tells about past records. It would tell them what they could expect if it came to an expensive fight. This wasn't out-and-out illegal but is not a part of a normal business procedure. It also wasn't recently added to business license application procedures.

The interesting thing is that though I objected at the time to the financial statement requirement, I did supply the information. No one raised any objections to any facts in the financial statement. Of course this makes sense if the purpose wasn't to check the specific facts of my finances but to see the size of my general resources.

What may have been most annoying was how my personal financial statement became public information. An e-mail I received from my attorney, Robert Hunt, indicated agenda items supporting the fact that the material became part of public information. The city's motives for asking for this information are easy to guess—scoping out their enemy—but I'm not sure about why they wanted to release the information.

Let's get paranoid for a moment. A personal credit check gives them enough information on my financial responsibility in the past. A personal financial statement lets Sky Trek and the city know how deep my pockets are, and how far I can fight them. The need for this becomes questionable. However, the statement gave them the information they needed. They now knew my pockets weren't deep enough to keep fighting for the project for more than a few months. Reading the financial statement, they knew they had a good chance of delaying me enough to make me give up. This was what actually happened.

Release of the financial statement publically had two possible explanations. One was sheer carelessness: never attribute to malevolence what can be explained by stupidity, as the old saying I've cited before goes.

Another explanation was the battle for public opinion. It was likely if I went away, I would just leave. But if there were any public controversy, the city could say it may not have handled things as well as it could have—admitting minor fault is always good PR—but the new fueling facility would have failed anyway. This guy Corbett lacked the money to carry it out.

Two interesting e-mails are quoted below. They were sent out a bit after the airport manager's letter.

April 8, 2008
Dennis Turner [city planner] to Nick Pinhey

I spent several hours today with Jerome on the fuel farm issue as I didn't feel comfortable with my grasp of the issues. As I did so, I began to believe that we have moved ahead of ourselves. Based on our current progress, I do not believe we should be moving this issue to EDC next week. I let Jerome know that we still had some work to do. About the same time Judy advised me that Wayne had some concerns and stopped the progress of the report review.

I've scheduled a meeting with Rick Corbett (MFC), Jerome and myself to discuss the project timelines, milestones and deliverables. At this point in time, the next thing we need to see is a fully developed project description from Rick. The city will then need to review that description to determine what level of environmental review will be needed. At that time we will have a better idea of how the project will develop and be taken to council.

I think the project has several complications that we need to work through to ensure fair and appropriate treatment of all involved. I also do not want to go to committee until we have answers to all of the questions we know will be asked.

Not there yet...

The same day, long before I saw the above e-mail, I sent a note to Bob Hunt:

Just a heads up: Michael Dye, an aviation business consultant I hired to do my business plan, has had a meeting with Jerome Thiele (airport manager) today at Modesto Airport. Apparently, what Jerry told him is that Sky Trek is going to come at me and the city with full force to prevent my opportunity to offer fuel services. Also, there are a lot of other discussions that brought up many flags that Michael felt were absolutely asinine.

Michael has been around for many years, and owns a Jet Center himself and can't believe what went on today with his conversations with Jerry Thiele. Jerry even mentioned to Michael that with what is going on and what is about to happen is the reason why there hasn't been another FBO on the field for the last 25 years. A statement that Michael couldn't believe came from an airport manager's mouth.

He is going to call you tomorrow morning to speak with you about what happened and what he feels is coming our way. I think it may be time to look into what is going on, and I really do feel that I'm being torpedoed for trying to expand my business, and muscled out. And everything I've witnessed, what Rich Pinnell witnessed, and Michael has witnessed, shows that Sky Trek has done everything to try to stop this.

On a side note, Jerry stated in the last two Airport Advisory Committee meetings that there is no Minimum Standards Agreement and that the policy that the airport has in place is the letter from the FAA. That letter states, in a few words, that not one business can have the exclusive right to provide aviation services to include fuel. This is the policy that the airport abides by and it is an FAA document. He read that twice in both meetings so that everyone was in the know including the owner of Sky Trek, who happens to be the chairman of the AAC committee.

Jerry has informed Michael that his boss wants to meet with me on Friday to explain what's going on and the 'political climate' that is involved. A sort of 'facts of life discussion' as he put it. Anyway, just to keep you posted. There was an opportunity to offer fuel and I went for it. I felt that I could expand my business and I can't believe the actions that are taking place.

I think this is the time I could use some help.

Chapter Nine
The Lawyers Jump In Full Force

On June 30, 2008, Modesto Mayor Jim Ridenour and airport manager Jerome Thiele got a long letter from attorney Michael L. Dworkin. Perhaps not realizing it, though lawyers tend to be careful, he delivered his message to the mayor and Thiele in the first two paragraphs:

> This office represents Sky Trek Aviation. As I'm sure you are well aware, Sky Trek has served Modesto Airport for over 25 years, eight of which as the Airport's sale fuel vendor. It has heavily invested in the Airport—having spent over $8 million in the purchase of one and construction of five hangars, the construction of a state of the art underground fueling facility (costing several hundreds of thousands of dollars, as required by the City) and the construction of other facilities and improvements.
>
> Approximately 65-75% of the total value of all aircraft based at the Airport (some $41 million), and which generate substantial tax revenues, are hangared or tied down at Sky Trek's facilities and depend upon the continued viability of Sky Trek's fixed base operation ("FBO"). Between the FBO operation, its hangar and tie down facilities and its

on-demand air charter business, Sky Trek employs 48 people.

Sky Trek is economically important to the City of Modesto, the letter said. The government, therefore, had a strong impetus to let them have their way on this and keep MFC from adding a fuel service.

Dworkin then went to specifics, along with implied and direct threats:

> The purpose of this letter is to express Sky Trek's serious concerns with MFC's proposed fueling facility at the Airport and the possible legal ramifications of approval, construction and operation of the proposed facility.

On the surface "legal ramifications" means allowing me to open my facility might have violated laws and regulations. Of course it also meant if I opened my facility, the city might have gotten sued.

Dworkin then summarized his case:

> This proposal falls short on several grounds:
> 1. A second fueling facility at the Airport is simply not viable in today's market;
> 2. The construction and operation of a fueling facility at the location proposed by MFC would violate the Airport Master Plan, which requires that all fueling facilities be situated in the Southwest corner of the Airport immediately south of the existing Sky Trek

fuel farm on an existing vacant parcel;
3. The construction and operation of a second fueling facility would violate FAA Grant Assurances in as much as the Airport has never established minimum standards, which are a prerequisite to additional Airport development;
4. The proposal, if implemented, would give MFC an unfair advantage in terms of both pricing and location, putting the Airport in breach of FAA Grant Assurances; and
5. The lease, construction and operation of a second fueling facility, without the requisite environmental reviews would violate the California Environmental Quality Act (CCEQA).

While *competition* at first blush may seem desirable, in this instance it's is merely a buzzword. Sole-source FBOs/fueling facilities are not necessarily anticompetitive and do not necessarily constitute the granting of exclusive rights. Airports like Charlotte International, Minneapolis-St. Paul International, Seattle/Tacoma International, Portland International, Birmingham International, Buffalo International, Sacramento Executive, and Kansas City Downtown, having far more annual operations than Modesto's 81,768 total operations in 2007, have only single FBOs.

Interesting, but there are a few things wrong with this argument. Some of the airports listed are not comparable to the situation at Modesto. And if they are, the situation there may also be wrong and in violation of the law, FAA regulations, and basic fairness. An analogy comes to mind of a robber who claims the court has to let him go because another robber wasn't caught.

How did the international airports get their fuel services? Did one just set up and drive out opposition? Or where bids solicited, with the lowest bidder—the best price—getting the contract? There is also the case, as discussed above, of using customer power to put prices down. A single pilot can put little pressure on a fuel supplier to keep prices reasonable. A major airline such as JetBlue can put on a lot of pressure. If, for example, prices are too expensive at Kennedy Airport in New York, there is a full-size international airport just across the river in Newark, New Jersey. Many other cities, such as Washington, DC, have more than one international airport relatively near each other.

The situation in Modesto is simply that with no competition, fuel prices were higher than they probably should have been. And as Sky Trek and its lawyers seemed to forget, competition doesn't mean it's a good idea to compete. There was virtually no chance a competitive situation would arise when MFC and Sky Trek destroyed each other. Even then we would not literally destroy each other. The city ensured if MFC went out of business, it would not leave an environmental mess. It also could have found a way to ensure viable facilities would be left for a city takeover.

If MFC prospered and Sky Trek went out of business, that would be life. If I went out of business, tough; that would also be life.

This interesting and entertaining (I am being sarcastic) letter continued. The lawyer was critical of the contents of a document he not only had not seen but didn't think existed:

We have not seen any business plan, submitted either by MFC or its fuel supplier, Conoco-Phillips, demonstrating a need for a second fueling facility and the economic viability of same, particularly in the present market. To the extent that any such business plan does exist, we question whether it fully addresses:

i. Present-day economic realities, i.e., the recent downturn in the economy and rapidly escalating fuel costs (for which no short-term, or for that matter, long term relief appear to be on the horizon) which are adversely affecting the aviation industry;

ii. The recent 30+% decrease in fuel sales from 2007 levels at Modesto Airport. This significant decrease will become even more substantial as a result of Sky West Airlines' suspension of Modesto-Los Angeles service. Prior to suspension of that service, Sky West accounted for 20% of all fuel pumped at Modesto;

iii. The dilutive effect it will have on the existing fuel Business at Modesto. Who are MFC's/ Conoco-Phillips' new fuel customers? Will they be attracting any new business to the Airport? We submit that MFC will be unable to bring in new customers or airport users and instead will poach ([sic!] competition is now poaching, it seems) existing airport tenants and Sky Trek's existing customer base. Put simply, the creation of a second fueling facility will not only substantially dilute the presently diminishing fuel market at Modesto, but adversely affect the existing level of service, as neither Sky Trek nor MFC will be capable of selling sufficient volume to justify their respective investments and costs of doing business;

iv. Potential anti-competitive and predatory results produced by MFC/Conoco-Phillips' efforts to penetrate the market, as we fear that they will substantially discount their fuel products below actual costs of production, distribution and sale in order to gain a foothold.

Unless and until these issues are addressed, we submit that any business plan, and any City review and/or approval of same would be woefully deficient. Moreover, any business not fully addressing these issues is destined to fail.

Virtually every complaint the lawyer had made so far was addressed by my documents, including the response documents that follow this section. But rereading this several years later, I still can't get over the focus on economics and whether my idea was good over and above legality. Was the lawyer supposed to raise just legal issues? Or was this letter both a strongly implied threat of a lawsuit and setting out economic reasons for the MFC proposal to be rejected? Look, the letter said to the Modesto city government that the MFC proposal, if approved, would hurt a politically powerful business. This could also have resulted in less tax income for Modesto.

The city may have looked at the implied worst case of MFC failing and destroying Sky Trek. However unlikely, it would not have been able to reject the possibility totally. So far in the letter, the lawyer was including legal threats, scaring the city with an equally hidden but equally implied appeal to public-spirited instincts—as if saying, "Don't leave the airport without fuel service."

I wasn't aware that under most circumstances a financial investment was required for an idea to be good, at least as far as government authorization. (Though my lenders and suppliers certainly could and should and did look at the economic viability of my plan). The government looking at the "good idea" was certainly not in keeping with free enterprise. There are exceptions, such as some Wall Street behavior in the past few years. However, my plan could have included some guarantees against failure and damage to the airport. Again, if I failed, that was my problem. In the unlikely event I drove Sky Trek out of business; that was their problem. I couldn't see any situation leading to the mutual destruction of us both. Ask yourself, did they see themselves unable to compete fairly?

The lawyer didn't forget legalities, turning to the airport master plan and adding a few more interesting turns of phrases and variations on logic:

> The Airport Master Plan does not authorize the construction and use of a fueling facility and does

not allow for FBO construction at the location which MFC has proposed. Further, such construction and use would be contrary to and in violation of the Airport Master Plan Master Plan, which specifically states:

"The Southwest Side of the Airport, adjacent to the county park, has been identified as the only remaining site for additional FBO facility development... (Master Plan at 7, emphasis added)."

While the Master Plan does not provide for...a second fuel farm, it does mandate that new facility development, such as that proposed by MFC, be constructed in the Southwest side of the Airport along the main apron. This was mandated by the City over 18 years ago when Sky Trek, at great expense, developed, constructed and commenced operation of its fuel farm; and to this date, neither the Master Plan nor the policies required by it have ever changed. In retrospect, had Sky Trek been permitted to do what MFC now proposes to do, i.e., build an above-ground facility literally adjacent to its front door, it would've saved a substantial amount of money and other resources.

Apparently an airport master plan, in addition to being carved in stone (or cement tarmac), does not allow for more up-to-date technology. As for location I would've been willing, if not happy, to compromise. Perhaps I should have stressed this more or called their bluff on this issue.

It seems, from the tone of much of this letter, that the master plan was written in stone and couldn't be amended.

Keep in mind also that the laws and regulations on environmental studies were apparently much less permanent.

The next issue was minimum standards. The FAA had *recommended*, not required, that minimum standards for different activities be established. One could say, "So, establish them." I would not have objected to meeting reasonable standards and never did object. But Sky Trek's lawyer tried to make the case to delay if not prevent my efforts, punishing me for either the judgment call or the errors of the Modesto airport management:

> Federal law requires that airport recipients of federal funding sign a grant agreement that sets out the obligations the airport must assume in exchange for federal assistance. The FAA has recommended that airports establish minimum standards as a means to minimize potential for violations of federal obligations at federally obligated airports.
>
> *FAA Advisory Circular AC 150/5190-7 provides, in pertinent part:*
>
> The airport sponsor of a federally obligated airport agrees to make available the opportunity to engage in commercial aeronautical activities by persons, firms, or corporations that meet reasonable minimum standards established by the airport sponsor. The airport sponsor's purpose in imposing standards is to ensure a safe, efficient and adequate level of operation and services is [sic] offered to the public.

Such standards must be reasonable and not unjustly discriminatory. In exchange for the opportunity to engage in a commercial aeronautical activity, an aeronautical service provider-engaged aeronautical activity agrees to comply with the minimum standards developed by the airport sponsor. Compliance with the airport's minimum standards should be made part of an aeronautical service provider's lease agreement with the airport sponsor.'

The FAA suggests that airport sponsors establish reasonable minimum standards that are relevant to the proposed aeronautical activity with the goal of protecting the level and quality of services offered to the public. Once the airport sponsor has established minimum standards, it should apply them objectively and uniformly to all similarly situated on-airport aeronautical service providers. The failure to do so may result in a violation of the prohibition against exclusive rights and/or a finding of unjust economic discrimination for imposing unreasonable terms and conditions for airport use. (AC 150/5190-7 Sec. 1.1)

The AC further states that airports should strive to develop minimum standards that are fair and reasonable to all on-airport aeronautical service providers and relevant to the aeronautical activity to which it is applied (Id, Sec. 1.2.a.), and that airports should:

1. Apply standards to all providers of

aeronautical services, from full-service FBOs to single-service providers;
2. Impose conditions that ensure safe and efficient operation of the airport in accordance with FAA rules, regulations, and guidance;
3. Ensure standards are reasonable, not unjustly discriminatory, attainable, uniformly applied and reasonably protect the investment of providers of aeronautical services to meet minimum standards from competition not making a similar investment;
4. Ensure standards provide the opportunity for newcomers who meet the minimum standards to offer their aeronautical services within the demand for such services (Id. at 1.2.d.).

The Airport has never promulgated minimum standards. As such, any granting of authority to engage in new and/or additional aeronautical activities on the Airport must undergo careful scrutiny to ensure that the granting of such authority is reasonable, not unjustly discriminatory, attainable, uniformly applied and reasonably protects those providers who have invested in the Airport and in Airport facilities consistent with market demand. We respectfully submit that the Airport has failed to do this.

Why is competition, as proposed in the MFC plan to expand to offer fueling services, unfair? Is it because I was taking advantage of new, less expensive but equally or more efficient and safe technology? Is it because MFC *might* have engaged in predatory pricing? There was no reason to believe this was the case unless one considers reasonable prices—lower than Sky Trek's monopoly prices—to be predatory. Saying I *might* engaged in activities that could easily cross the line into illegal is also a curious argument for a lawyer to make in a public document with no evidence. Could I have sued him for libel?

Was it because it was a better location? If Sky Trek beat my prices or even matched them with its reputation as an established service, people would still go to them. But read the section of the lawyer's letter untitled "unfair advantage":

> Granting the subject proposal would create an unfair advantage for MFC and unjustly discriminate against Sky Trek in violation of (i) the Airport Master Plan, (ii) Federal Grant Assurances and (ii9) FAA-recommended minimum standards.
>
> The Airport Master Plan provides, in pertinent part:
>
> FBOs which offer basic services, e.g. fueling, maintenance and flight training, they are to be highly visible and have access to major taxiway and airport access roads. To the extent possible these conditions should be equal for each FBO leasehold... the general pattern of services for small aircraft is expected to remain much as it currently exists... (Master Plan at 61-61 [emphasis added]).'
>
> In addition, the Airport, which has received

Federal Airport Improvement Program ("AlP") funds in the past and is currently seeking more funding on other unrelated matters, is contractually bound to Federal Grant Assurances, among them Grant Assurance 22(c), which provides:

Each fixed-based operator at any airport owned by the sponsor shall be subject to the same [terms] as are uniformly applicable to all other fixed based operators making the same or similar uses of such airport and utilizing the same or similar facilities.'

The Airport required that Sky Trek build an underground facility in the Southwest comer of the Airport, which Sky Trek did at substantial ($395,000) cost. MFC's proposed facility will consist of two large above-ground storage tanks on skid mountings, a far less costly alternative.

While the Airport no longer requires underground tanks (we have yet to see these published standards), the substantial savings in building an above-ground facility will create an economic windfall for MFC, while at the same time diluting Sky Trek's fuel business. More importantly, however, is the location of the respective facilities.

Sky Trek's facility is in the Southwest comer of the Airport, as required by the Master Plan, outside of the traffic lanes between the runways and hangars. Even if there was no predatory pricing by Conoco-Phillips or MFC, the proposed facility's more central location would make it more attractive to aircraft owners and operators, resulting in diversion and dilution of Sky Trek's fueling

> business.[2]
>
> Sky Trek is a full-service FBO, providing aircraft tie-down and storage, maintenance, transient services and facilities, conference rooms and ground transportation, in addition to its fuel service and aircraft charier business. Many of the services and facilities that Sky Trek provides to aircraft owners and operators and other Airport users are at little or no compensation and Sky Trek essentially relies upon fuel revenues to subsidize these services and facilities.
>
> MFC isn't an FBO. As reflected in it Notice of Proposed Construction or Alteration, dated December 19, 2007, all that it wants is the right to dispense and sell fuel, essentially "cherry picking" and providing little in return. Essentially, MFC is requesting the Airport's consent to an operation that, as constituted, will harm the current airport environment, dilute or destroy current airport revenues and frustrate the long-term investment that Sky Trek has made in the Airport.

Realistic predictions of the service I was planning to offer said my proposed service had an excellent chance of increasing total services. Even the Sky Trek lawyer, in the same letter from which I'm quoting, accused me of preparing to "poach" clients from Sky Trek—in other words the airport would still keep the total clients and total income, just from a different source.

Finally Mr. Dworkin pulled out his big gun: the environmental study. It's next to impossible to argue against protecting the environment. Public opinion may gloss over one company doing better than another company but will show little sympathy to a company that seems not to care about the environment. The lawyer actually quoted legal precedents—previous cases that supported his opinion. My main counterarguments were always that a formal and expensive study wasn't required, but there would be environmental reviews at all stages of construction of my proposed fueling facility.

The letter continued:

> Lastly, MFC's proposed fueling facility is a project under CEQA, which requires that an environmental assessment be conducted before proceeding.
>
> All local agencies must prepare an environmental impact report on any project that they intend to carry out or approve which may have a significant effect on the environment; Berkeley Keep Jets over the Bay Com v. Board of Port Co, 91 Cal. App. 4th 1344 at 1354 (2001). California Public Resources Code #21065 defines "project" as an activity which may cause a reasonably foreseeable indirect physical change in the environment, and which involves the issuance to a person of a lease, permit, license, certificate, or other entitlement for use by one or more public agencies.
>
> An environmental Impact report ("EIR") should be prepared 'whenever the action arguably will have an adverse environmental impact.' No Oil, Inc v. ell) of Los Angeles, 13 Cal. 3d 68 (1974). CEQA is to be interpreted in such a manner as to afford the fullest possible protection to the environment, Friends of Mammoth v. Board of

Supervisors, 8 Cal 3d 247 at 259 (1972).

While an EIR was conducted originally for the Airport Master Plan, that Plan didn't address a second fueling facility, let alone one at MFC's proposed location. In Laurel Heights Improvement Assn. V. Regents of University of California, 47 Cal 3d 376 (1988), the California Supreme Court held that an EIR is inadequate if it fails to discuss the anticipated future uses of a planned facility, and the likely environmental impacts of those uses.

An EIR must be created to review the environmental impact of a second fueling facility should MFC's plan go forward. Presumably, in order for two fueling facilities to be economically viable, there must be an increase in the amount of fuel sold, which would require a dramatic increase in the number of aircraft operations.

From where will these additional operations come? What, if any environmental effects are caused by such additional operations…?

Did the lawyer think two fueling facilities could be "economically viable," and that this could relate to "a dramatic increase in the number of aircraft operations"? So my proposed fueling service ran a risk of damaging both Sky Trek and the environment from to much additional business for both of us? This whole thing would've been entertaining if I hadn't had so much at stake and been so personally involved.

With two more paragraphs, Michael Dworkin brought his document to a seemingly reasonable end:

> For the above reasons, Sky Trek Aviation opposes the MFC proposal. There is no demonstrated need for a second fueling facility and its effects would be economically devastating for Sky Trek, the Airport and eventually Airport users. However, to the extent that the Airport deems a second facility necessary or desirable, the Airport should require that MFC provide a full-service FBO facility on the Southwest side of the Airport consistent with current Airport Master Plan requirements.
>
> If the Airport is unwilling to adhere to this requirement it must initiate appropriate actions to amend the Master Plan and promulgate fair and equitable minimum standards to (i) permit the MFC project and (ii) concurrently permit Sky Trek to build an above-ground facility in a central-location at the Airport and recompense Sky Trek for the remainder of its present underground fuel facility's useful life.

This was a curiously reasonable idea. I wonder why nothing came of it.

Anyway, the lawyer continued:

> Sky Trek's management and this office would be amenable to meeting with Airport and City officials to further explore alternatives that would better serve the interests of the parties, the Airport and its users.
>
> In the interim, as this matter is presently scheduled for the July 8, 2008 City Council meeting, it

is requested that the City Clerk include copies of this letter in the packets that will be distributed to members of the City Council in advance of that meeting.

This letter pretty much spoke for itself, despite my giving in to the tendency to add comments. The letter, meant to stress legal reasons against opening my fueling center, began with basically reminding the city of what Sky Trek had done for the airport and the city. I'm guessing this included campaign contributions. It spent more time on general economics than legality. The lawyer said he doubted I submitted a full-fledged and comprehensive plan—why the firm didn't ask for such a plan in its letter to Jerome Thiele, I don't know. The March letter gave the distinct implication that he and Sky Trek had a source of inside information. Virtually right after saying he wasn't sure a plan existed, the lawyer stated what was probably not in this nonexistent plan.

The lawyer spent a lot of time on the unfair competition MFC would offer Sky Trek, including using what might have been described as *new technology*—secure, above-ground tanks. The lawyer said MFC would damage Sky Trek economically, even leading to a situation where the airport had no fuel service. But in the final section, the lawyer stated the increased business necessary for both companies to prosper might have proven environmentally damaging, though he had just finished saying there wasn't enough business.

The lawyer threw a lot of issues into the mix, perhaps searching for a winner or just being sure everything was mentioned in case of later legal proceedings. Was this lawyer setting it up so he could cherry pick arguments later, to use in a formal legal procedure?

I think the two main points of the letter were the opening paragraph reminding the Modesto government of Sky Trek's influence and the call for an expensive environmental study.

A response to the Dworkin letter was prepared soon afterward and submitted.

It is worth quoting in full:

> General Comments:
>
> Hendley-Sky Trek lease dated February 21, 1989, 4.d states, "This Airport Lease shall not be construed to be an exclusive Lease or concession, and LESSOR shall have the right to deal with and perfect arrangements with any other individual, firm or corporation engaging in like activity from the Federal Grant Assurances."

I would've liked direct access to the lease—"best evidence," as the lawyers called it. But for the purposes of this book, the Sky Trek lease specifically stated the Modesto airport could contract for the same service with another firm.

The response continued:

> 22.Economic Nondiscrimination
>
>   a. It will make the airport available as an airport for public use on reasonable terms and without unjust discrimination to all types, kinds and classes of aeronautical activities, including commercial

aeronautical activities offering services to the public at the airport.
b. In any agreement, contract, lease, or other arrangement under which a right or privilege at the airport is granted to any person, firm or corporation to conduct or to engage in any aeronautical activity for furnishing services to the public at the airport, the sponsor will insert and enforce provisions requiring the contractor to:
1. Furnish said services on a reasonable, and not unjustly discriminatory, basis to all users thereof;
2. Charge reasonable, and not unjustly discriminatory, prices for each unit or service, provided that the contractor may be allowed to make reasonable and nondiscriminatory discounts, rebates, or other similar types of price reductions to volume purchasers.
c. Each fixed-based operator at the airport shall be subject to the same rates, fees, rentals, and other charges as are uniformly applicable to all other fixed-based operators making the same or similar uses of such airport and utilizing the same or similar facilities.
d. The sponsor may establish such

reasonable and not unjustly discriminatory conditions to be met by all users of the airport as may be necessary for the safe and efficient operation of the airport."

The somewhat odd numbering refers to the Sky Trek contract. The contract and regulations seemed to call for basic fairness for both sides. I never asked for anything different.

The document then dealt with exclusive rights, the heart of the issue.

23. Exclusive Rights

It will permit no exclusive right for the use o/the airport by any person providing, or intending to provide, aeronautical services to the public. For purposes of this paragraph the providing of the services at an airport by a single fixed-based operator shall not be construed as an exclusive right if both of the following apply:
    a. It would be unreasonably costly, burdensome, or impractical for more than one fixed-based operator to provide such services;
    b. If allowing more than one fixed-based operator to provide such services would require the reduction of space leased pursuant to an existing agreement between such single fixed-based operator and such airport.

> It further agrees that it will not, either directly or indirectly, grant or permit any person, firm, or corporation, the exclusive right at the airport to conduct any aeronautical activities, including but not limited to: charter flights pilot training aircraft rental and sightseeing, aerial photography, crop dusting, aerial advertising and surveying, air carrier operations, aircraft sales and services, sale of aviation petroleum products whether or not conducted in conjunction with other aeronautical activity, repair and maintenance of aircraft, sale of aircraft parts, and any other activities which because of their direct relationship to the operation of aircraft can be regarded as an aeronautical activity; and that it will terminate any exclusive right to conduct an aeronautical activity now existing at such an airport before the grant of any assistance under Title 49, United State Code.

The airport had two fuel providers prior to 1988.

> Eighteen years as sole operator—[Sky Trek's] ability to recover cost of development—Airport tenants have not enjoyed benefits of competition. Is MOD GA population small due to lack of competition over the years?

Sky Trek started small and grew over the years.

> Lease on fuel farm for 35 years. Threat of lawsuit from Modesto Flight Center if not allowed to move

forward.

Alas, the Modesto government had already seen my personal financial statement and knew I would probably not be able to fund a lawsuit.

Five focus areas:
1. A second fueling facility at the Airport is simply not viable in today's market. References to other airports that are larger but have just one FBO.
Business decision by Modesto Flight Center—Business Plan looks out three years Business Plan submitted May 19, 2008—reviewed by City Finance May 27-31. 2008—58 pages, requested March 14, 2008.
Minneapolis-St. Paul used to have two FBOs, south side and west side prior to 1986.
[Modesto] Airport has lacked competition for 18 years. Airport hangars full—building new hangars—Airport to market new hangar lease opportunity—City and County population has grown—strong historic trend.
Per Mr. Corbett, Sky Trek has kept self-service fuel prices low for several weeks, creating an environment where the new MFC fuel facility will be marginally profitable for the near term.
2. Construction and operation of a fueling facility at the location proposed by MFC would violate the Airport Master Plan.

> Master Plan is a living document that can be amended/updated. Master Plan similar to City General Plan - it cannot anticipate all future development opportunities Airport sponsor has to keep Airport Layout Plan up-to-date …new ALP will include location of proposed facility.

As they used to say in the 1960s, right on! The master plan was a living document and could and should have been kept up to date.

> 3. Lack of Minimum Standards—the Airport has never promulgated minimum standards Recommended by FAA, not required Minimum Standards are living documents—can be modified (OFAA). One recommendation on commercial minimum standards (AC 150/5190- 7)…"minimum standards are optional…the FAA does not approve minimum standards…will review proposed minimum standards."
> March 9, 1994 letter, Howard Cook, airport manager…MOD proposed Minimum Standards submitted to FAA.
>
> 4. The proposal would give MFC an unfair advantage in terms of pricing and location and discriminate against Sky Trek.
> Sky Trek has enjoyed 18 years without competition. Both firms propose to operate

mobile fuelers to capture business. MFC will not be permitted on North ramp leased by Sky Trek. Exxon sign up for 18+ years. Proposed new direction sign.

How much business is self-service? How much will Sky Trek lose? Conclusion: all questions raised in the Dworkin letter point to efforts to delay project.

I couldn't have put it better myself.

I received an interesting letter from Jim Thiele in early July 2008. As my lawyer put it in his response: "We are in receipt of your request to our client that he supply you with information regarding his position relative to locating his fuel facility adjacent to the existing Sky Trek fuel facility."

The lawyer responded that I was opposed for the following reasons:

1. The FAA has stated that the [initially planned] location was fine.
2. All of our client's plans, specs and specifications including our lease, our contractor's quotes and the build out requests are based on the present proposed location for our new fuel facility.
3. The present location is, in part, for the use of Modesto Flight Center, its customers and transient aircraft. It will cost Modesto Flight Center additional maintenance costs and employee costs to shuttle an aircraft back and forth between the Modesto Flight Center

facility and the fuel facility, if it is located adjacent to the fuel facility for Sky Trek.

4. It will be more convenient for the customers of Modesto Flight Center and transient aircrafts to refuel at the present proposed location for the new fuel facility and to attend events hosted by the Modesto Flight Center. Sky Trek's facility has been located at its present location for 20 years. In fairness, Modesto Flight Center should not have to locate it facility adjacent to the facility of Sky Trek.

5. Given the present location for the new proposed fuel facility, Brad Wall, of the planning department has stated that Modesto Flight Service does not have to do any CEQA for the proposed location.

6. The Airport Advisory Committee approved the proposed site for the proposed fuel facility, as did the FAA.

7. Sky Trek leases the small shack right in front and to the right of Modesto Flight Service. In effect, if Modesto Flight Service is required to locate its fuel facility next to Sky Trek an unfair and disadvantageous would be created for Modesto Flight Service. Sky Trek could set up a line station at the above described shack and have a fueler standing by.

8. In order to create fairness to both parties, Sky Trek should be allowed to post signs directing aircraft to its fueling facility.

It didn't seem like I was offered an agreement in exchange for changing the location of my proposed facility. But Thiele was sounding me out. Or he was seeking a compromise? I was never offered one. And am I imagining that all compromises in this whole question would have been likely to cost me a lot of money?

Let's get paranoid for a moment. The waiver of the CEQA environmental study, for all the good it did me, was issued for the original location. I'd have avoided if I'd changed plans. Anyway, on July 2, 2008, both the discussion and approval of my plans were pulled from the City Council meeting.

Chapter Ten
Meanwhile, Back at the Environmental Study

One advantage of text messages is they may make it easier to trace events and establish a timeline through saved messages. But some of the people involved in this process were old-school folks who used landline telephones to talk to other people. Documents went out via e-mail. My lawyer's letter to Jim Thiele was dated July 3, 2008. The next document in sequence, the next event, was an e-mail dated July 22. Things had apparently been busy in those three weeks. For one thing Sky Trek had previously been planning defense, countering my arguments and offering arguments of their own. They went over to offense in July.

On July 22, 2008 I e-mailed my attorneys:

> "We normally try to pay our fuel bill with Sky Trek monthly and in payments. They have been doing that for many years. But, without notice today, or any warning, they ceased fueling of our aircraft. The accounts department said that the owner wants us to pay in full if we want them to continue fueling operations. This, again, was without any warning or heads up to prepare. Needless to say, I had to put $20,000 on a credit card just so I can continue my operations.

> "I offered to pay $11,500 just to get my balance current through June and get us operating, and they declined, saying it must be paid up to last week. No warning, no heads up; just ceased fueling operations for us. We were crippled today for a few hours. It was unbelievable.
>
> "If subtleness does not work, Sky Trek would be obvious. Shut down the opposition. Kind of makes me think of scenes in gangster movies where the store owner resists paying protection and gets some of his merchandise broken.

I also mentioned the latest with the environmental study.

> On another note, I spoke with Jerry Thiele, the airport manager. I asked him that we had an environmental person and wondered who we needed to ask if this person was adequate. He said he would call me back on an answer. When he did, he was so frustrated because what he told me on Friday changed and now, according to Raleigh Stevens [Actually Roland Stevens, city attorney. I got the name wrong] we can only go through a city inspector because they want full control over what he/she does. Raleigh didn't [want to risk] any chance of being sued by Sky Trek. It sounded like Jerry Thiele was getting pretty upset and frustrating at the actions be taken.

Two city e-mails on the same day confirmed my e-mail. To show what careful thought they gave to the issue, Thiele e-mailed Stevens at 3:45 p.m. He got an answer all of six minutes later. Stevens said:

> The objection is that we lose control of the study is he used his guy, and the outcome will be a foregone conclusion. The City could get sued in CEQA by Sky Trek and incur defense costs, etc., because Corbett's environmental work isn't sound. The deal should be that we do the environmental work (or our consultants, as the case may be) and Corbett pays us for our costs…

Looking at this from the perspective of two years later, I wonder why the city didn't offer to do the work itself and just charge me for time and expenses. City workers are cheaper than outside consultants. Have I answered my own questions?

The city's whole idea, as it became clearer and clearer, was to delay me and wear me out. Perhaps the papers got lost, or perhaps this was agreed to verbally. There was a whole lot of circumstantial evidence but so far no smoking gun. To mangle an old saying, I heard quacking, saw web-footed prints, and I was being suffocated by feathers. But the ducks all remained carefully hidden. How do you get your ducks in a row if you can't even see them and new ones keep showing up?

For example a brand-new duck appeared in August 2008. I suddenly needed a federal NEPA (National Environmental Policy Act) study. There was now a clear focus on the environment, with Sky Trek's business needs at least temporarily in the background. This was well done—I'm speaking sarcastically—on the part of my opponents. Protecting the business interests of a company is less appealing to the public than protecting the environment.

The public was less likely to understand any subtle details of the legal requirements for environmental studies or my objections to the issue suddenly appearing as the city reversed its previous decision. Stressing Sky Trek business success as the objection to my proposal made it look like a bully with control over the government trying to protect its pocketbook.

Keep in mind the documents in which these issues were stressed weren't meant to be made public. Stressing the environment makes the city and Sky Trek look like good guys.

Speaking of good guys, on July 30 my lawyer sent me an interesting e-mail. He was told by city officials that they felt they were "doing us a favor by making approval of your facility absolutely bulletproof," to enable it to stand up against any Sky Trek lawsuit. Stalling so much that I would likely give up and not build the facility also made it bulletproof against a lawsuit. With friends like the Modesto City government, you don't need enemies!

And merely delaying a decision, not rejecting my proposal, made it much harder—as I learned the hard way—to appeal. I was learning a lot in this process and not enjoying it.

A few days later I expressed my frustration in an e-mail to Rich Pinnell of Ascent Aviation Group, my partner in the proposal:

> So I get off the phone with Dennis Turner a bit ago, and he basically informed me that there is no way that I can be on the August 12th date [for the City Council meeting]. Of course I asked why. Apparently due to the fact that the CEQA is being requested on an airport, that we also have to

have a NEPA (national environmental policy act) requested as well.

And since now they don't have a qualified person to do both, they had to go out and search for one. They located such a person and will chat with Dennis regarding quotes. Now...the timeline...Dennis told me that this will take at least two months, because there is a point where they list the request in a public forum for comments, critiques, objections, etc. which the NEPA consultant will have to address each statement.

Dennis feels that Sky Trek will capitalize on this opportunity. He felt remorseful and told me that he can understand my frustration. He also applauded my professionalism by doing everything that the city has asked of me to do and without hassle. BUT this has to be the last straw.

1. Why is this being requested now and not months ago when they requested a business plan from me?
2. Why does it seem suspicious that a letter from Sky Trek's attorneys was a motivating factor to have me removed at 6 am on a Friday before a three-day weekend and a day from my original July meeting?
3. Why is a private entity involving itself in this process to block me from having a fuel facility added to my business?
4. How can I find someone responsible for lost revenue for something that should have

been requested months ago, but is now being requested after Sky Trek's attorney's letter?
5. Why do I have to pay for a consultant that the city chooses, while I have no say in the matter? Where is this in writing that states that a CEQA and a NEPA is required at Modesto Airport? Where are any of these suspicious activities that have occurred since I submitted my request in writing?
6. Should I remind everyone that the initial delay from Sky Trek's attorney was to delay the first AAC meeting?
7. What about the fact that the owner of Sky Trek was head of that committee and voted for a delay?
8. How about the request of a business plan for my proposal that included my fuel operations, and also, something entirely unrelated, my helicopter operations? That also had to include my PERSONAL FINANCIAL STATEMENT! What regulation and legal guidance required me to do a business plan?

As a private entity, I can't believe of the unfair treatment I have received since day one. Everyone in this email has been involved in some way or another regarding this process. At what point do we say enough is enough? At what point do we state that there were ethical violations of an appointed position of the AAC?

At what point do we state that an outside entity

can't directly interfere with the improvements of another entity? At what point do we state that the city is being manipulated and lobbied (been told that) to not allow the approval of fuel facility proposal?

At what point do we allow an outside source to manipulate city officials to pull my item off the agenda the day before a three-day weekend, at which I was scheduled to be on the following day? And in fear of a lawsuit from Sky Trek? At what point does my lender for my fuel facility decide to walk away and I have no loan because of all the delays?

And finally, at one point is the law ever *on my side?*

I ended my e-mail with, "Sorry for the rant."

Rich Pinnell seemed to agree with me. "This is crazy... If this is allowed to go on, no one would be able to install a fuel farm." That was the idea.

It's petty to complain there was still no indication Ascent would help with legal expenses. They weren't the party at fault.

Chapter Eleven
Summaries of Process and Progress

An Outside Summary of the Process

An August 17, 2008 letter from a general aviation expert consultant company called Business Presentation Solutions provided an excellent summary of the immediate situation in response to a request from my lawyer. The primary purpose of the letter was to provide an opinion and guidance for the lawyer. This letter was purely objective, since it wasn't intended for publication.

Realistically the letter appears in this collection and in the official material used for my case and protests because it is very favorable to my position. This letter confirms what I'd been saying and thinking throughout this process. My lawyer had asked an outside expert what he thought about what was going on. The expert didn't think much.

To be honest, this document, intended as background for my lawyer to prepare the letter that follows, would not have seen the light of day—at least not from my end—if it didn't support my position. But it could've come to light in a lawsuit in what is called a *discovery*, where the opposing lawyers ask for all documents on a subject or issue. The letter from the Sky Trek lawyer to Jerome Thiele, discussed earlier, seemed to have had the curious effect of being treated like a discovery even though the lawyer only requested specific documents. The letter from the outside consultant follows:

> This is in response to your request for my opinion with respect to the ongoing conflict between Mr. Richard Corbett, who owns the Modesto Flight Center ("MFC"), and the City of Modesto ("the City") over MFC's intent to expand its commercial aviation operations to become an approved Fixed Base Operator ("FBO") at the Modesto City-County Airport ("the Airport").
>
> The events of the last several months seem to indicate that MFC's progress has been purposefully delayed by the City as a result of political pressure and illegal wrangling by MFC's competitor, Sky Trek. It is clear that Sky Trek's intent is to block MFC's competition which, in and of itself, is a violation of the Federal Aviation Administration's Grant Assurances, as a result of the exclusivity that Sky Trek has achieved.
>
> The matter is exacerbated by the Airport's (and the City's) inability to clearly and effectively manage what should have been a fundamental (and routine) process for the approval of expanded services by a well-known commercial aeronautical operator, like the Modesto Flight Center. At a federally-funded Airport of Modesto's size and stature, given the circumstances, MFC's approval should have been a "no-brainer," with a timeframe of no more than 120 days from start to finish.
>
> In my experience, this type of behavior is

common in communities across the country where a City or County attempts to operate their Airport "in a vacuum" with the belief that the best course action for dealing with a proposer like MFC is a political one which can effectively bar competition and promote discriminatory practices. However, this is exactly the type of behavior that is frowned upon by the FAA, who looks at an airport's management as the on-site entity that is responsible for representing the FAA's ultimate interests, and avoiding discriminatory practices with respect to commercial aeronautical operators. After all, the FAA is really the owner of the Airport's infrastructure and the City is the custodian.

Such is the reason for normal policies and procedures that should be in place in the Modesto Airport's administration that would assist them in dealing with MFC's application.

Clearly, City officials have given Sky Trek's argument (which was stated in a letter dated June 30, 2008 from Sky Trek's legal counsel to both Airport and City officials) top priority over the Airport's management personnel, and have allowed the company to create concern over several non-issues that should have been dealt with by Airport management quickly and effectively early in the process. Several of these issues are discussed in the following:

Issue NO.1 - CEQA Approval: In the aforementioned letter, the issue is raised by Sky Trek's counsel that there is a need for a CEQA review to approve/disapprove the installation and placement of Sky Trek's fuel farm. The City's response was to immediately cancel MFC's appearance at the City Council meeting (just three days away) on July 5 without any justification or notice to MFC, its owner, or legal counsel. The cancellation was issued for the third time in several months.

It is clear that the City has not followed a set of *administrative* procedures that would *effectively* facilitate the process which MFC is entitled to as a commercial aeronautical operator at the Airport. Moreover, through its influence Sky Trek has successfully sidetracked the process. The Airport's approval process should have been designed to protect MFC, but has been discriminatory instead. A synopsis of the critical *events* which make Sky Trek's argument *ineffective* in this regard follows:

In May of 2008, MFC submitted a comprehensive Business Plan to the Airport (and City) which *provided* a detailed description of the Modesto Flight Center's plan for expansion into a full-service FBO. The content of that plan clearly answered any and all questions that were required by the Airport/City in their letter dated May 15, 2008. At that time, MFC was assured by the Airport and City Staff that there were no outstanding issues (including environmental *review* and recommendation to proceed) that would delay the process.

Subsequently, MFC was *given* a draft of a lease and operating agreement which integrated *its* existing operations with the additional leasehold and operating rights that would be necessary to expand its operations into that of a full *service* FBO. MFC *viewed* this positively and was assured that the process was *moving* forward.

Subsequently, MFC was *advised* that the City's environmental staff had inadvertently failed to submit a letter indicating their findings that no CEQA *review* was required. Subsequently, MFC's first Council appearance (scheduled for early June, 2008) was cancelled and delayed for a month because the City's staff had not provided the proper letter of approval.

However, on June 9, MFC was allowed to appear before the City Council's Economic Development Committee ("EDC"), which is a preliminary step in the process of approval by the City Council. After a brief discussion by the members, the EDC voted favorably and forwarded its recommendation for approval of MFC's project to the City Council. It should be noted that neither Sky Trek nor its council were present to provide any discussion at the EDC meeting. Subsequently, MFCs appearance was scheduled for July 5, 2008. This was a clear indication by the Airport management that all was in order and that the process was moving forward.

As previously mentioned, subsequent to the EDC's favorable vote and recommendation, MFCs appearance at the full City Council meeting was cancelled without notice or discussion as a result of Sky Trek's June 30 letter. MFC believes that this letter was timed to effect further delay.

Analysis: Clearly under any normal circumstances, *the process* of MFCs approval should have been allowed proceed to the City Council for a vote. Questions about CEQA had already been answered by City staff, and the airport manager's recommendation should have been to allowed proceed, with Council approval (and MFC's project start-up) contingent upon the fulfillment of any and all required permitting (including CEQA, if required). Normal procedure should have been followed.

Issue No.2 - Sky Trek's "Viability" Argument: On page 2 of Sky Trek's letter, their counsel discusses five (5) points in which the MFC proposal "falls short on several grounds."

My response to their argument follows:

- *Additional Fueling Facility:* Sky Trek's argument that an additional fueling facility at the Airport is "not viable" is simply their opinion. Statistics seem to indicate that the majority of general aviation owners, operators, and users on the field will actively support such an installation and that competition will be welcomed, since Sky Trek's main facilities are located on the opposite side of the Airport. This is further referenced by the letters of recommendation that MFC submitted to the City along with its Business Development Plan.

- *Violation of the Airport's Master Plan*: The Airport's Master Plan is a *planning* document that is over eighteen (18) years old and which provides the Airport and users with a roadmap for long-term use, development, and operational projections. Accordingly, it isn't intended to be a document which doesn't allow the Airport (or the City) to deviate when new opportunities or situations arise that can be beneficial or promote growth and development, especially since it has not been updated in the recent past. This is the case with the Modesto Flight Center's FBO expansion proposal in that it provides the Airport and its users with a full-service operator and facility on the west side of the Airport.
- *Minimum Standards/Violation of Grant Assurances*: Sky Trek's argument is unfounded here, since the application of minimum standards is "optional" according to FAA Advisory Circular AC150/5190-7. A strong argument can be made that the situation as it currently exists is discriminatory and has prevented competition from challenging Sky Trek in the past. Further, it is clear as to why Sky Trek didn't participate in the development of minimum standards before this point, since such would've created a mechanism for additional competition.
- *Unfair Advantage-Location*: It is unclear as to what "advantage" MFC will have from its location on the Airport, since Sky Trek's original

operations were in the same location as MFC is now and they opted to build their present facilities and infrastructure on the opposite side of the Airport.

Clearly, Sky Trek has had ample opportunity over the years to continue expansion of its operations (and to provide a more prominent presence on the south side of the field), yet has not done so. From the users' perspective, MFCs planned facilities and operations will provide them with a useable, visible, and state-of-the-art fuel farm that is designed to support the 100+ based aircraft that are located there and the transient aircraft from the region who wish to use it.

- *Unfair Advantage for Pricing:* This is a dangerous argument for Sky Trek, since it has always had an advantage in setting prices and is now complaining about potential competition.

Analysis: After a review of their argument, it is clear that Sky Trek is concerned about MFC's competition and is actively seeking to protect their status as the "exclusive" FBO at the Airport by using the FAA's minimum standards as a shield. This, however, isn't how the FAA intended their minimum standards guidelines to be interpreted.

In fact, the *PC 150/5190-7* states that the Airport can't establish any new rules that would *prohibit* the offering of new services. This is especially true as it relates to an FBO business that is as large and viable as Sky Trek, in an Airport market that is arguably between 600,000 to 900,000 gallons annually (with continued growth potential).

From the FAA's perspective, the fundamental goal of the Airport and its service providers is to ensure that the Airport's users are offered services and facilities that will encourage the Airport's use at all levels. MFC, through its on-going operations as both a user and a service provider, understands this concept and has stepped forward to offer the level of products, services, and facilities that are in demand the Airport's users. Moreover, in MFCs experience, Sky Trek's fueling operations are woefully inadequate are not designed to support the users on the south side of the field.

Issue No.3 - Sky Trek's Conflict of Interest: There is ample evidence of discriminatory practices because of the situation in which Sky Trek's has been given a place and is allowed to be a voting member (and current chairperson) on the Airport's Board.

Analysis: This is readily recognized as a significant conflict of interest, in that it affords him the capability to act in a role of approval over any potential competitors that may be seeking the Board's blessing or approval. Moreover, it is unfathomable that Sky Trek would be granted the right to question a potential competitor, or have access to proprietary and confidential information such as business plans, financial statements and projections, market planning, etc.

It prompts me to recommend that Mr. Corbett or you should review the Board's Charter (which should be found in the State's records) to insure that no laws have been violated by the situation.

In summary, I believe that your course of action is clear with respect to the discriminatory practices that have occurred:

1. This issue is not about an Airport that is not viable or is constrained by location of low fuel volumes. My opinion is that that you must actively press City officials to move forward with approval of MFC's right to operate, even if such approval is conditioned upon reasonable parameters (all of which have been previously approved). Clearly, Mr. Corbett is supported by the majority of the Airport's users, he has received an approval letter for the placement of the fuel storage facility from the FAA, and he has the Business Plan in place that will enable him to move forward with this viable project. MFC's record is enviable in that it is a large flight school with a dozen aircraft and numerous professional affiliations and a viable aircraft maintenance operation, which includes both fixed and rotor-wing aircraft, that has been in business over 27 years.

    Even in the absence of minimum standards, I believe that although the Airport and City have moved to support MFC, through their administrative actions they have unjustly discriminated against Mr. Corbett by allowing Sky Trek to delay the process without any justification or legal grounds whatsoever.

2. Given the foregoing, it is my opinion, after an extensive study of the intent of the FAA's minimum standards over the past 20 years, that the FAA should be contacted for a meeting to examine the situation as it relates to discrimination against MFC and perhaps others in the past.

The Modesto Flight Center is exactly the type of commercial aeronautical operator that the FAA encourages and supports, and I would be greatly surprised if you were told otherwise. MFC's track record over the past year is strong evidence against Sky Trek's argument of doom and gloom, in that Mr. Corbett and his staff have successfully grown and improved the company in very challenging times. If I were in Sky Trek's position, I would be afraid of the intense competition that Mr. Corbett will eventually bring to the Airport in the coming years.

Thank you for the opportunity to express my opinion and view on behalf of Mr. Corbett and the Modesto Flight Center. Feel free to contact me if you have any additional requests or comments.

Sincerely,

Michael L. Dye

Business Presentation Solutions

The key in this extensive and careful analysis is: "If I were in Sky Trek's position, I would be afraid of the intense competition that Mr. Corbett will eventually bring to the Airport in the coming years." This may be stating the obvious and certainly reflects my views.

After having the chance to read the letter, my lawyer sent a strong summary of my case to the city, dated August 27, 2008, addressed to Mayor James Ridenour and the six members of the city council. I still hoped something could come of my proposal, but in retrospect I think my efforts were already doomed by the time this letter went out:

> We represent Richard Corbett and Modesto Flight Center in reference to obtaining a lease for additional fuel service facility at the Modesto Airport. Mr. Corbett has been attempting to obtain a lease from the City and establish his fuel facility since December 11, 2007. More than eight months have gone by and this matter has yet to be submitted to the City Council for hearing and approval.
>
> In December of 2007, Mr. Corbett started the procedure to obtain a lease from the City for installation of a fuel facility. At the present time, Sky Trek operates the only aviation fuel facility at the airport. At the time, Mr. Corbett was told by Jerome Thiele, airport manager, that "we anticipate taking approximately 90 days from start to finish."

Please see Mr. Thiele's letter to Mr. Corbett dated December 11, 2007...To date, Mr. Corbett has yet to receive approval from the City for a proposed ground lease for the fuel facility.

It was not until May 15 of 2008, that Mr. Corbett received a letter from Mr. Thiele...The letter was written more than five months after Mr. Thiele represented that the entire approval process would only take 90 days. As you can see from the letter from Mr. Thiele, the requirements placed upon Mr. Corbett were, to say the least, onerous. Among other things, Mr. Corbett had to provide a one-year consolidated financial statement. We question the need for the financial statement, and we remain concerned about publicly disclosing Mr. Corbett's personal financial information.

As was pointed out earlier, I wouldn't have objected if the approval process had taken a few more than ninety days, but at the time of this letter it had taken about twice that. The personal financial statement remained stuck in my craw, so to speak. Why did the city need such information? I still concluded a credit report, though usually sufficient, would only have told them about my credit record, not how much money I had in the bank. Releasing it publically may have been mere carelessness, but it also fit the pattern. Were they trying to embarrass me publically or set up justification for turning me down if the issue became public?

We call your attention to a letter from the Federal Aviation Administration dated May 1, 2008...the

Federal Aviation Administration indicated they do not object to the construction of Mr. Corbett's proposed fuel facility at the airport.

On June 9, 2008, the subject of Mr. Corbett's request regarding a fuel facility land lease was on the agenda of the Economic Development Committee. At the time of the meeting of the Economic Development Committee; the City of Modesto staff recommended that a lease agreement be negotiated with Mr. Corbett and that it be presented to the City Council for approval. All three members of the Economic Development Committee voted in favor of the staff's recommendation.

We attach a copy of the memo...from Nicholas Pinhey, Public Works Director, to the Economic Development Committee. A summary of Mr. Corbett's endeavors to obtain permission from the City Council for a lease and to proceed with establishing an aviation fuel facility at the airport is contained in the memo from Nicholas Pinhey, the Public Works Director, to the Economic Development Committee under the heading 'Background.'

By letter to the City Council dated June 23, 2008, Brad Wall of the Planning Department confirmed that a California Environmental Quality Act (CEQA) investigation was not required...

This matter was scheduled for hearing before the City Council on July 8, 2008. On July 3, 2008, the Mayor, the City Clerk and Mr. Thiele received a letter from attorney Michael Dworkin which is dated June 30, 2008. Mr. Dworkin represents Sky

Trek. According to Assistant City Attorney Roland Stevens, Mr. Dworkin's comment about the need for an environmental assessment was the only comment that concerned Mr. Stevens. Without the courtesy of a telephone call to us or our client, the hearing on this matter before the City Council was dropped.

This confirms what I was thinking and the arguments offered in response to Dworkin. The economic arguments against my project were basically that the MFC fueling facility might have caused economic damage to Sky Trek. Though this would have been of concern to Sky Trek's management, it wasn't relevant. I don't see how the city could take into account the potential for illegal or unethical business behavior on my part. But if I outcompeted Sky Trek, that would be the free enterprise system in action. And other evidence was that most of MFC's fueling income would likely have come from expanding the market, not "poaching" Sky Trek clients. If I had the chance to outcompete them, they had the chance to outcompete me.

Following the unilateral removal of this matter from the July 8th City Council agenda, Mr. Stevens informed us that it would be necessary to prepare an environmental assessment. We were told by Mr. Dennis Turner of the Department of Public Works that a consultant would be retained to investigate the environmental impact of our client's proposed fuel facility and prepare a report. Our client was not allowed to have any input into selection of the consultant, but according to Mr. Stevens, our client will be required to pay for the report.

Almost two months have passed since this matter was dropped from the agenda of the City Council. To our knowledge, the City has taken no further action. That is, a consultant has not been retained to investigate this matter as it may affect the environment. The undersigned has had two to three conversations with Mr. Stevens regarding this matter.

While Mr. Stevens feels that a CEQA investigation is necessary, nevertheless, Mr. Stevens has not been able to clearly explain to the undersigned why such an investigation is necessary. We do not share our client's concerns regarding City employees; nevertheless, he is concerned about the input that Sky Trek may have had leading to this matter being dropped from the City Council calendar and his efforts to obtain a lease being stonewalled for months on end.

That was a curious line about city employees, apparently referring to their objectivity. I wonder if the lawyer was playing "good cop" (him) and "bad cop" (me) at this point.

Relative to the above-ground tanks that Mr. Corbett proposes to install, enclosed you will find a proposal from Garsite. You will note that the proposal "contemplates the sale to Modesto Flight Center of two 12,000 gallon tanks"…The tanks are Underwriter Laboratories approved…Not only are the tanks UL-approved, the tanks meet the requirements for "protected" tanks as defined by the National Fire Protection Associations Rule 30 (NFPA).

As you can see from the enclosures, the above-ground tanks are certainly safe and pose no threat to the environment. In fact, the tanks proposed are safer and more compatible with the environment than the underground tanks presently in place and used by Sky Trek.

I still believe a formal and expensive environmental study wasn't legally required, nor was it necessary. But I think I could've passed, were it possible for the study to have been done—and had it been done objectively.

Two further paragraphs from the above dealt with support for the proposed fueling facility from the Modesto Airport Pilots Association and mentioned my intention to provide fuel for Angel West flights (taking patients for medical treatment) at cost.

My lawyer continued:

> We enclose an advisory circular...from the Federal Aviation Administration dated January 4, 2007 and entitled "Exclusive Rights at Federally-Obligated Airports." As we understand it, the City receives grants from the federal government for maintenance and improvement of the Modesto Airport. The above mentioned advisory circular provides, among other things, that:
> "It is FAA policy that the sponsor of a federally obligated airport WILL NOT grant an exclusive

right for the use of the airport to any person providing, or intending to provide, aeronautical services or commodities to the public and will not either directly or indirectly, grant or permit any person, firm, or corporation, the exclusive right at the airport to conduct aeronautical activities.

"The exclusion prohibition applies to both commercial entities engaging in providing aeronautical services and individuals. The intent of the prohibition on exclusive rights is to promote fair competition at federally obligated public use airports for the benefit of aeronautical users. The exclusive rights prohibition remains in effect as long as the airport is operating as an airport even if the original period for which an airport sponsor was obligated has expired."

Sky Trek Aviation has enjoyed a monopoly as a fuel provider facility at the Modesto Airport for approximately 20 years. An unnecessary delay in approving a lease to Mr. Corbett and Modesto Flight Center for a fuel facility furthers the monopoly that Sky Trek now enjoys. By promoting that monopoly, the City of Modesto jeopardizes the grants it receives from the federal government.

We enclose for your review Section 21083 of the Public Resources Code…We also enclose California Code of Regulations Sections 15064 et seq…It is obvious that it must be shown that there would be a significant effect on the environment by the proposed project. By the way, we also question whether or not the installation of above-ground fuel tanks can be considered a project.

Again, Section 21083 of the Public Resources Code provides in part:

"The guidelines shall specifically include criteria for public agencies to follow in determining whether or not a proposed project may have a significant effect on the environment."

Section 21068 of the Public Resources Code defines "significant effect on the environment" as a substantial or potentially substantial adverse change in the environment.

We also call your attention to San Joaquin Raptor/Wildlife Rescue Center vs. the County of Stanislaus (1996) 42 Cal.AppAth 608 and Davidon Homes v. City of San Jose (1997) 54 Cal.AppAth 106. The courts have held that when an agency has determined that a proposed project comes within one of the exempt classes, this necessarily includes an implied finding that the project has no significant effect on the environment.

Where an agency establishes that the project is within an exempt class, the burden shifts to the party challenging the exemption to show that the project is not exempt. See California Code of Regulations, Title 14 section 15300.2. In other words, once the City determined that Mr. Corbett's proposal was exempt, the burden was upon a challenger to show the possibility of an adverse environmental impact sufficient to remove the project from the categorically exempt class.

My attorney then cited California Code of Regulations' Section 15061. He was particularly interested in (b)(3):

> The activity is covered by the general rule that CEQA applies only to projects which have the potential of causing a significant effect on the environment. If it can been seen with a certainty that there is no possibility that the activity in question may have a significant effect on the environment, the activity is not subject to CEQA.
>
> The above provision is commonly known as the "common sense exemption." This exemption was adopted to guard against the possibility of an obviously exempt project not listed in the category of exemptions from being required to comply with the requirements of CEQA. The common sense exemption is discussed in Myer v. Board of Supervisors, 58 Cal.App.3d 413 at 425.
>
> Pursuant to CEQA, a "project" has two elements. First, it is an activity that may cause a direct (or reasonably foreseeable indirect) physical environmental change. Second, it is an activity that is directly undertaken by a public agency, an activity supported in whole or in part by a public agency, or an activity involving the issuances by a public agency of some form of entitlement or permit. It is submitted that Mr. Corbett's proposal is not a project, since it will not have a significant effect on the environment. See our discussion above. The tanks comply with NFPA-30 and are approved by the Underwriter Laboratories. Please see Public

Resource Code 26083 cited above.

We ask that the City Council apply the "common sense exemption" in this matter. In doing so, the exemption letter written by Mr. Wall should prevail. See Public Resource Code 21083 cited above.

We also call your attention to the California Fire code, Title 24, Part 9, Sections 1106.1 et seq., 2201 et seq., and 3404.1 et seq. This section refers to aircraft fueling. The code section cited above determines what need be done in order to provide a safe environment. Further, it is our understanding that Mr. Corbett's proposal for a fuel system has been reviewed by the Fire Assemblies. Certainly, Mr. Corbett's proposal complies with the Fire Code.

Finally, we call your attention to correspondence from Tamorah Bryant, P.E., an Environmental Engineer...Ms. Bryant has concluded that:

"In a situation such as proposed construction of an aviation fuel storage tank and refueling assembly on an existing airport site, where the proposed activities meet the requirements of NFPA-30 and Section 1106 of the California Fire Code and no other unforeseen issues are present on site, it is my opinion that a finding of significant environmental impacts would not be likely."

There is no doubt that the National Environmental Policy Act (NEPA) does not apply to the proposed lease nor the proposed fuel facility to be built at the Modesto Airport by Modesto Flight Center and Richard Corbett for the following reasons:

1. The Federal Aviation Administration (FAA) has approved the proposed aviation fuel facility to be built by Modesto Flight Center and Richard Corbett. The approval by the FAA certainly implies that the FAA didn't consider NEP A to be applicable to the construction of the proposed facility.
2. The courts have held that NEPA does not apply [unless the] proposed action significantly affects the quality of human environment. The courts have also held that, in determining whether or not there is a significant effect on the quality of the human environment, the reasonable standard is to be applied.
3. Federal Courts have construed the word 'major' with the word 'significant.' Applying the reasonable standard, the proposed fuel facility will have no significant effect on the environment.
4. ...the action of the FAA in approving the proposed fuel facility requires compliance with NEPA only if it changes the environment. If the environmental status quo will be maintained by an agency, the environment is not considered to be effected for the purposes of NEPA. It appears Sky Trek already has a fuel facility at the airport, so the fuel facility proposed by our client is certainly much more environmentally friendly. Accordingly,

the proposed fuel facility will not change or affect the environment.
5. For NEPA to apply, agency acts (approval by FAA) must change the physical environment and subsequently harm a person. In applying the reasonable and the common sense rule, it can't be said that the proposal of our client will change the physical environment and subsequently harm a person.

On another subject, we would like to mention that the City of Fresno has approved the installation of a new aviation fuel facility at the Chandler Airport. The approval was made without the necessity of a CEQA report.

Clearly the political situation was different in Fresno. Maybe I should've looked there for my flight school and fueling center. Fresno has over twice the population of Modesto, about 500,000 people—it's the fifth-largest city in California and smaller than LA. But neither Fresno nor Modesto is a small town, though Modesto may think and act the part.

It is not necessary that City departments conduct further investigation into this matter before the Council's consideration for the following reasons:

1. Mr. Corbett has complied with all requirements of City personnel.
2. A Statement of Exemption was in fact issued.
3. The tanks in question have already been

pre-approved by Underwriter Laboratories and Rule 30 of the National Fire Protection Association.
4. Applying the common sense rule, the double-walled, above-ground tanks approved by Underwriter Laboratories and the National Fire Protection Association do not present a hazard to the environment.
5. Since a Statement of Exemption has been issued, the burden now shifts to anyone who opposes Mr. Corbett's proposal to establish that there would be a hazard to the environment.
6. By allowing a monopoly to continue at the Modesto Airport, the City is placing in jeopardy its continued receipt of federal grants for the airport. As we have pointed out above, a monopoly is forbidden by the United States Codes and also by the Regulations of the Federal Aviation Administration.

In short, it appears that the principals of Sky Trek are attempting to influence the City of Modesto in order to maintain their monopoly at the Modesto Airport. Because of the delay in approving the lease for Mr. Corbett, he is losing a great deal of revenue. Those who oppose Mr. Corbett's project for their own financial interests clearly hope that Mr. Corbett will run out of funds to build his fueling facility before the lease is approved.

The real argument was an attempt to appeal to the council's sense of fairness. By this point this was perhaps a bit naïve for both my attorney and me.

> It is in the best interests of the City of Modesto and the Modesto Airport to have competing fuel facilities at the airport. Open competition is always good for a community and for its economy. For the good of the community and to avoid in any way jeopardizing federal grants for the airport, it is requested that the City Council approve the lease that was to be presented to it on July 8, 2008, in order that Mr. Corbett may proceed to build his fuel facility.
>
> It is absolutely ludicrous to contend that this matter is subject to any kind of CEQA review. Not only are the tanks approved as indicated above, but in addition, the installation of the tanks will be subject to obtaining appropriate permits and must meet with requirements set forth in...Mr. Wall's letter of exemption...There can be no impact on the environment because of the installation of a fuel facility by Mr. Corbett.

A good letter, but we'll see what its ultimate effect really was.

Chapter Twelve
More About the Environmental Study

On September 8, 2008, in a letter signed by airport manager Jerome Thiele, I was officially informed that a California Environmental Quality Assurance (CEQA) review would be necessary and that a National Environmental Protections Act (NEPA) study might be necessary. I was also informed that a consultant would have to prepare the study and that I would not be permitted to choose the consultant.

> Thank you for your interest in doing business at the Modesto City, County Airport. As discussed with in a recent phone conversation Dennis Turner, we have been advised by the City Attorney that a California Environmental Quality Assurance (CEQA) review will be required for your proposed fuel facility project. Your proposed project may also be subject to review under the National Environmental Protections Act (NEPA). The City Council can only act on your proposal after all environmental requirements are met.
>
> The City Attorney pointed out that we were mistaken in assuming that the lease agreement, required for the development of an aviation fueling facility, would not trigger a CEQA

review. We regret that this error has cause a delay in the processing of your proposal. However, the Airport/City has a legal requirement to complete all required steps, including the CEQA review, prior to a determination being made on your proposal.

As the agency responsible for ensuring the integrity of the CEQA review process, the City retains primary responsibility and control over such reviews. There is not an option for you to hire a consultant to meet this requirement. However the costs associated with the review are your responsibility as the project proponent.

We have obtained proposals from several qualified consultants and have selected one which we believe will move the process forward as quickly as possible. The consultant has proposed a cost of $18,970 assuming no NEPA work is needed. Should a NEPA document need to be prepared to the level of a Notice of Intent (NOI), there would be an additional cost between $1,500 and $8,800.

The consultant estimates a timeframe of five (5) week to complete the scope of work. If you choose to proceed with your proposed project, we will need payment of $18,970 before the work can be initiated. You are advised that these types of projects sometime require additional work as determined by the review. These would be additional costs you would be required to pay before the review and conclusions could be completed.

The proposals that were received in response to our request are available for your review if you so desire.

You have asked when this item can move forward to the Council for consideration. We will be prepared to go to the first available council date after the review and subsequent findings and documentation have been received and reviewed by city staff.

The day this letter was sent, Jerome Thiele received an e-mail from the FAA notifying him that I had filed a complaint. Two days after that, on September 11, my lawyer sent a request for documents to the City of Modesto Public Works Department. He basically asked for everything relevant. What he couldn't get were documents that didn't exist—fully verbal conversations where the powers that be laid down the law. What my lawyer also couldn't get was instances where a lower-level person anticipated what might have been wanted and acted, or failed to act, on his or her own initiative.

I received some press after that. *The Modesto Bee*, the local newspaper, ran a front-page article on me on September 12, 2008. In it my attorney, Charles Brunn, alleged the city was trying to run me out of business.

This was denied by city attorney Susana Alcala Wood. She said city employees had first believed it would not require a CEQA study but then changed their minds. As Wood put it, "[We] realized it might require a higher level of scrutiny, just before Corbett was scheduled to appear before the City

Council in July." Wood is quoted as saying, "Sometimes we catch things and then we have to say, 'Let's make sure it's done right.'"

I'm described in the article as tracing the city's change of mind to the Sky Trek attorney's letter of June 30, 2008, which I discussed earlier. This raised economic issues. But it also raised the environmental study issue. The economic issues seemed to have been put in to remind the city of Sky Trek's contributions and as a "just in case" if they had to raise the issue in a lawsuit.

I thought the letter's coming only a day or two before the decision was more than a coincidence. The city attorney denied they were acting to protect the Sky Trek monopoly. The article then had a very interesting paragraph:

> [City attorney Wood] said Sky Trek's June 30 letter wasn't the only factor that persuaded her office to require that Corbett hire a consultant to investigate whether he'd have to do a more thorough environmental study. She said the attorney's office was leaning that way before it received the letter.

So she claimed the letter, from the representative of an anything but disinterested party, was only part of the reason for their decision. This was confirmed by an e-mail about a week later from my attorney. The city attorney "did say that there has been an objection and therefore a preliminary study was necessary." Had there been no such objection, would my plan, which was potentially dangerous to the environment, have been allowed to go through without an environmental study?

My proposal wasn't brought before a formal city council vote, but the issue was raised.

At the September 23 city council meeting, members of the community, the president and treasurer of the Modesto Airport Pilots Association (see their letter of support in the appendix), and my attorneys gave testimony on issues that had occurred during this entire process. Members of the community gave testimony that Sky Trek had been fuel gouging the local pilots for many years. They testified that was why the general aviation community didn't fuel up at Modesto if they could help it.

Sky Trek was clearly taking advantage of the fuel increases in 2008, when their prices were more than those at a major international airport twenty minutes's airtime away (San Jose International Airport). A member of the city council didn't like what he heard and ordered an investigation into the wrongdoings and delays; he was "very concerned about stonewalling" throughout my proposal and about how the city manager had to report back to the city council.

I never received notice of the findings and am not aware if that investigation was ever done. The city council felt there were shortcomings in the process and they wanted a report on it; again I never received confirmation it was accomplished, let alone a copy of the report.

The September 23, 2008 presentation by one of my lawyers got mixed reviews. The first came from Gerald Braun, the son in the father-and-son attorneys representing me:

> By now, you've probably heard from Julie regarding the City Council meeting last night—Dad's passionate presentation was well received.
>
> Council members were very concerned about the stonewalling, and they ordered the City

Manager to report on the delays and their causes.

Charlene gave an articulate presentation regarding the need for competition. Rogers' partner said his attorney had told him to say nothing, but "we just want to be on an even playing field." This is a sign of things to come. At a future hearing for the approval of the lease, Sky Trek will whine about their investment in the airport, and about how unfair it is for a newcomer to step in and start a fuel facility without making a similar investment. We're ready to counter such BS!

City Attorney Wood said that her outside attorney expert on CEQA/NEPA opined yesterday afternoon that a study was necessary. She had already provided the council members with a copy of the FAA email, below.

Bottom line, the council directed the City Attorney to move ahead as quickly as possible with the required environmental review. The City will not pay for the review…you will be required to pay.

The attorney continued with some practical advice gleaned from what he evaluated as a mixed-bag council meeting:

> My professional opinion/advice? Let's keep the pressure on Wood and Dennis Turner this week. They believe the cost of the environmental study will be greatly reduced now that the FAA has narrowly defined the scope of any study. Depending on the cost of the study, the best course of action may be to pay for the study and get it done. The

> council is sympathetic, but it's clear they are not taking action until Wood tells them the environmental issues are resolved.
>
> Other alternatives? File an action for a writ of mandate. Resolution, though, will take a long time, and will be more costly than the environmental study.
>
> Dad or I will let you know when we have heard from Dennis Turner about the revised cost of the study. If you and Julie are willing to pay for it, Wood has promised to get us on the Council agenda for approval of the lease in six weeks or less.
>
> So, it's a mixed bag. Our appearance last night "primed the pump," and in retrospect it was absolutely necessary to keep things moving. If we had not appeared last night, the City would've continued to stonewall. The council will be on our side, particularly Will O'Bryant. However, we will have to work with the City Attorney on the environmental study or file a court action. I suggest we see what develops by Friday afternoon before making a decision.

The need for an environmental study was becoming more and more settled, though the early FAA decision that a study was needed seemed to have narrowed the scope of the study. The scope would grow again somehow.

My FBO consultant, Michael Dye, had some different thoughts on the presentation before the City Council:

> As you may know by now...Colleen and I watched

the webcam of the meeting from my apartment in Harrison. At a point in time, I was totally incensed because of Charlie's inability to present. I was even angrier when I found out from Julie (my wife) that Jerry had made Julie stay in her chair and not speak.

I am not/was not impressed with Charlie's presentation (you can see it soon because they will have it in the archives at access TV); he left out several major points, and he is definitely not anywhere near forceful enough. It's easy for me to say, but last night was the time to stand and deliver, and he definitely was forced out of the goal by the City Attorney.

Here are some of the points I believe he should have made:

- He clearly should have used words like 'conflict of interest' when he was talking about the City requiring an $18,000 payment for the NEPA study and then demanding that their environmental person be used.
- He doesn't understand that the Airport and its environment should be treated differently than land that a common 'developer' would be utilizing.
- He had no grasp of the fact that Modesto is just a common landlord.
- He should have had the list of Cities that have installed fuel farms in California at his fingertips, with a question as to why Modesto

demands this when others don't.
- His explanation of the timeline was rambling—they lost interest quickly, and basically didn't give an f--- by the end of the discussion.
- I believe that he should have been a great deal more confrontational. I can now see why he thinks I'm too aggressive.
- Everyone lost sight of the fact that the Council is approving your land lease.
- An even greater point should have been made about the fact that these circumstances are in direct violation of the FAA's Policies for Airport, and that a Title 16 suit is imminent. Charlie made mention at one point that no one wants to get into lawsuits…what a dumba--. Typical attorney…wants to keep the billable time going.

And my thoughts to Julie are that once you have a chance to view the webcast, I would tell them that they will not get paid because they can't, and didn't deliver when the time came.

As for the FAA woman…I want to give her a call within the next couple of days and ask why her interpretation of the regulations are different (seemingly) than everyone else's (the other Airports who have installed). I need the backup documentation, though maybe Pinnell can provide me with this.

Also, I think it would be important to get hold of Lopez, one of the Council members, and attempt to discuss this with him. He seemed like he was pissed about the situation."

I'd hired the Brunns a few months earlier, at the advice of my attorney, Robert Hunt.

Hunt told me I needed to retain a local attorney in the Modesto area, one who might be tuned in to the political climate. I retained Gerald Brunn from Brunn and Flynn. Over the course of this entire process, from the point where it started to get ridiculous to the point we closed, the Brunns, which included Gerald Brunns's father, Charlie, appeared to battle it out with the city. But for the $65,000 bill I received from them over the course of less than seven months, you can see the results I received. I got a lot of bark from these attorneys but no bite. I wish this had occurred to me at the time, or at least after the September meeting.

On November 13, 2008, I filed a formal complaint with the FAA through my lawyer. That lawyer wrote to the FAA:

> This office represents Richard Corbett in connection with his attempts to install and establish an aviation fueling facility at Modesto Airport in Modesto, California. Mr. Corbett initially applied for this project on or about December 11, 2007. Despite assurances by airport manager Jerome Thiele that our client's project would be processed and approved in a timely fashion, OUI client has been mired in a bureaucratic morass. We are informed and believe that the City of Modesto has delayed our client's project for anti-competitive purposes in violation of the FAA Advisory Circulars

150\5190-6 and 150\5190-7 and the Airport Grant Assurance.

Sky Trek Aviation is currently the only supplier of aviation fuel at Modesto Airport. John Rogers, an owner of Sky Trek Aviation, is the chairman of the Modesto Airport Advisory Committee. Mr. Corbett's request to install an aviation fueling facility to compete with Sky Trek should have raised immediate red flags regarding Mr. Rogers' position.

Despite an obvious conflict of interest, Mr. Rogers insisted on chairing the initial advisory committee meeting on January 16, 2008, during which Mr. Corbett's project was considered. At this meeting, Mr. Rogers trivialized and mocked our client's proposed project, at one point even stating 'go ahead and amuse us.' It was only sometime after this meeting that Mr. Rogers excused himself from the decision making process. After Mr. Rogers excused himself, our client's proposal was approved by the advisory committee, and we were informed that his proposal would move forward to the City Council for approval.

Our client's project was also issued a CEQA exemption by Brad Wall of the Modesto Planning Department (See Exhibit B). In a letter dated December 11, 2007, the Modesto Airport manager Jerome Thiele promised our client that the entire approval process for his project would take approximately 90 days...Despite the advisory committee's approval of the project, there was no further response from the airport manager until Mr. Thiele sent a letter dated May 15, 2008... In this letter Mr. Thiele requested that our client provide...a personal financial statement for the previous year, a request that was never adequately explained to our client. Despite the odd nature of this request, our client complied in order to keep the process moving.

On June 9, 2008, the Modesto Economic Development Committee reviewed Mr. Corbett's proposal. The City of Modesto staff recommended that a lease be negotiated with our client and that it be presented to the City Council for approval. All three members of the Economic Development Committee voted in favor of the staff's recommendations, and the proposed lease was scheduled to be reviewed at a hearing scheduled on July 8, 2008.

Despite the initial determination by the Planning Department that a CEQA investigation was not required, our client was later told the exact opposite. Sky Trek's attorney, Michael Dworkin, had apparently written a letter to the Mayor of Modesto, the City Clerk and the airport manager, Mr. Thiele, wherein he raised various issues regarding the proposal, including a CEQA review. The scheduled hearing for July 8, 2008, was dropped without notification to our client. We were informed by an assistant city attorney, Mr. Roland Stevens, that an environmental assessment would be required, despite a presumption of the validity of the initial CEQA exemption, according to California Code of

Regulations, Title 14, § 15300.2.

This office has attempted to informally and formally resolve this matter with the City of Modesto. It was explained to all the relevant parties involved that our client's proposal would have no environmental impact. The proposed project entails the installation of two above-ground 12,000 gallon tanks which fully comply with pertinent federal and California State safety provisions. There is no need for a NEPA or CEQA review because there is no reasonably plausible environmental impact on any level.

Any concerns limited to the installation of the tanks and the operation of the fueling facility are controlled and regulated by federal and California State guidelines, specifically the California Fire Code. There is no associated impact on the surrounding environment, any projected increase in airport activity, or any other related commercial activity due to our client's project. The proposed project will merely provide a competing fueling facility for Modesto Airport.

We believe that the issue of competition is at the heart of this problem, not any adverse environmental impacts. A cursory review of the proposal would reveal Sky Trek Aviation is exercising undue pressure on the City of Modesto and the relevant parties involved to ensure retention of a monopoly. John Rogers, the owner of Sky Trek Aviation, sits on the advisory committee board and only excused himself from this decision making process after displaying unabashed hostility towards our client's project at that initial meeting.

Our client was then required to provide personal financial information, which has absolutely no bearing on the project at hand. We fear that his personal financial information was used to determine our client's capacity for pursuing this matter legally. Also, despite the initial letter of exemption from CEQA, the City reversed itself immediately upon receipt of the letter from Sky Trek's counsel.

The City's conduct is in blatant violation of Advisory Circular 150\5190-6 and 7 which forbid the granting of exclusive rights. 5190-6 states:

"The granting of an exclusive right for the conduct of any aeronautical activity on federally obligated airport is generally regarded as contrary to the requirements of the applicable federal regulations, where such exclusive rights result from an express agreement, from the imposition of unreasonable standards, or by any other means."

Also, Paragraph C, Part 22 of the Airport Grant Assurance, forbids economic discrimination. Part 23 forbids exclusive rights for "any person providing or intending to provide aeronautical services to the public."

Despite our repeated attempts to informally and formally resolve these issues, our client's project has not moved forward since February of 2008. Consequently, we request under 14 CFR 16 that the City of Modesto be issued a compliance order and required to profess and approve our client's proposed project in a timely and diligently [sic] manner.

Chapter Thirteen
The Last Hurrah

I sent a final e-mail to the city on December 4, 2008, addressed to city attorney Wood:

> In response to your November 14 letter that stated a timeline for the CEQA study to be started in the month of December and concluded approximately June 2009, Modesto Flight Center would like to start the process of the environmental report. The deposit that you mentioned of $5000 is ready to be applied towards the project.
>
> I am a little perplexed at that fact that stated in your November 14 letter, you still didn't know the estimated cost of the CEQA/NEPA, but "would have something early next week." Well, it has now been three weeks since you were supposed to send us a quote. Nothing has been received…again. This has been indicative to this entire process since the beginning my proposal back in November 2007. Why another delay?
>
> Now, you brought up the figure of $18,000 for the study, but you alluded to the fact that that number is not fixed and you 'consistently advised that you couldn't guarantee it.' But back in an email

sent to my attorneys and to Nick Pinhey, Dennis Turner, and Jerome Thiele on September 23, from the recommendation of FAA you commented: "It is possible now that with this suggested focused scope that the costs for the review will be reduced, I just don't have that information available right at this time. Staff can follow up with the consultants if you would like." This was back on September 23, and I never received a quote then. Why? Again, another delay.

At this moment, I do have some questions that I would like answered. I understand back on September 23 at the City Council meeting, Council Member Will O'Bryant and others "were very concerned about the stonewalling," and they ordered the City Manager to report on the delays and their causes. Furthermore, the council directed the City Attorney to "move ahead as quickly as possible with the required environmental review."

After discussion with the City Council's office this week, I come to find out that it wasn't until mid-November that a "closed-door" session took place and the determination of a time line was drawn up by Dennis Turner and delivered to the City Manager's office for it to be reviewed. I currently have a time-line that spans almost 1,000 pages from the inception of this proposal, which began on November 17, 2007 and which includes the results of a Freedom of Information Act request and all the email correspondence throughout this process.

My first question is: how can I see the timeline that Mr. Turner produced? I would like to compare it with the multitude of documents I've retained that detail the unnecessary delays that I've encountered throughout this ordeal.

I also understand that the closed-door session may have determined the time-line of the CEQA/NEPA study. My concern is the length of the study. Brad Wall has briefed us that the timeline typically takes twelve weeks to accomplish a CEQA/NEPA. So, why nine months? And is that the worst case?

So, to review, I have waited for a lease since November 2007. It is now December 2008 with no lease, no environmental review started, and no one that can give a good reason why.

Since January 2008, Sky Trek has raised their fuel prices higher than any area airports within 45 miles. In wasn't until the September 23 City Council meeting that they were openly accused of possible fuel gouging. The very next day, Sky Trek lowered their prices almost 60 cents, and after careful review, lowered their price even further to being the cheapest in the region. It wasn't until they were called out in public that they reduced their pricing.

But throughout the summer, I had to endure full retail pricing above and beyond even what pilots from even San Jose Int'l airport had to pay. With [Sky Trek] intentionally meddling in my proposal to install the fuel farm, to raising their fuel prices to beyond reasonable levels, Sky Trek has put a serious financial hardship to our company. Remember, throughout this entire process from November 2007 through June 30, 2008 there was never a mention that a CEQA was required from the city. It wasn't until Sky Trek's attorneys sent a letter to the city days before the July 8 City Council meeting, conveniently timed to where I couldn't appeal or contest, that the city decided to yank me from the agenda.

Bottom line, I feel that the city has let me down from multiple errors and inconsistencies throughout this process. The city has constantly delayed me time after time, adding onerous requirements to adhere to in order to get my lease. At the same, the city allowed the owner of Sky Trek, John Rogers, to chair the Airport Advisory Committee and didn't advise him to step down due to conflicts of interests and ethical issues during the early phases of my proposal. I feel the city has allowed Sky Trek to manipulate the process through multiple requests and objections from their attorneys.

Attached are two photos taken (video is available as well) on October 24, when my chief pilot noticed a very large spillage occurring at Sky Trek's below ground self-service facility. He felt that it had to be occurring for at least an hour and if he wouldn't have seen it, then this leak would've continued for who knows how long. The airport fire department was dispatched shortly thereafter.

I understand the process that I have in regards to my permitting. But shouldn't the city be more alarmed and concerned about Sky Trek's situation, due to the fact that the Tuolumne River is just over 100 yards and a residential neighborhood is about 75 yards away? My above-ground tanks would pose no environmental hazard, due to the leak-proof technology and double-wall construction. In the meantime, Sky Trek has aged below-ground tanks, with aged piping above and below ground, within yards of a major waterway and residential neighborhood.

What would the California Environmental Protection Agency think about that? I have to endure multiple delays and various "concerns" about a proven protected system that we are going to install.

I understand the financial/political clout that Mr. Rogers may have and the fear of a lawsuit that put some folks in a knee-jerking fear-state; that coming from an internal email that I obtained. But that still doesn't allow for a tenant on a federally-funded airport to be treated the way I've been for the past thirteen months.

Just think for a moment. I applied for a lease back in November 2007 and have done all of the arduous requirements detailed on a letterhead from Jerry Thiele that was required by me to fulfill for the lease approval back in May 2008. It is December 2008, and I've yet to even get my lease approved by the City Council.

Does that seem right? Isn't there something wrong here?

I've requested a meeting with the City Manager next week, and hopefully I don't have to go on an Air Force Reserve trip during that time, because I would like to discuss what has occurred throughout this process. I also would like to request that the CEQA/NEPA be done as soon as possible and let's see if we can get a shorter time-line on this. Additionally, I would like a price for this report.

Please stop the delays on this. This is unfair, and I've a right to know how much I am paying for this study. And furthermore, just because you use the excuse that the city has not said "no" to our proposal, the fact that there have been countless delays in my quest to receive a lease shows a protection of a monopoly on a federally-funded airport. And with this, an exclusive rights violation occurs when the airport sponsor excludes others, either intentionally or unintentionally, from participating in an on-airport aeronautical activity, such as aviation fuel services.

I understand there are probably those that would like me to simply "go away." But I'm not going to! I've a right to continue my process and receive the fair treatment I deserve. Please follow up with answers to my questions and a price tag for the CEQA/NEPA report.

By the way, I noticed on the bottom of your letterhead that it states in italics, 'Citizens First!'

How ironic is that?

The End of the Process

In mid-December 2008, after we sent the final e-mail to city attorney Wood, I began the thought process that led to the painful decision to close the flight center. Michael Dye was unable to come up with a suitable buyer/investor, we had mounting debts from fighting from the city, fuel prices were unbelievable, and we were in the dead of winter. There was nothing to do but close the doors and walk away. But I didn't want to do it around Christmas; I didn't want to do that to the employees. I'm not like that. I decided to make it January but wasn't sure when.

The eventual date was January 29, 2009. There was no other reason but I thought we had to do this and make it happen. Looking back, though, and perhaps thinking a little too much like a businessman, I wish it had happened on December 31. It would've made it much easier for taxes and other filing issues.

I gave up the fight for the fueling service on January 27, 2009 and Modesto Flight Center, Inc. closed two days later on January 29, 2009. This was a result of multiple contributing factors, some of which were economy-based while others dealt with fuel price gouging at Modesto Airport during the summer of peak fuel prices and the constant delays placed upon me by the City of Modesto during my process to obtain a lease for a fuel farm.

Chapter Fourteen
The Process in Retrospect

The Modesto Flight Center did everything the city requested along the way. The city would constantly state they were awaiting a $5,000 deposit check to do the CEQA study. They hid behind this statement even though I kept telling them no one would send a nonrefundable check to an entity not knowing the ultimate true cost of the project. That's like writing a blank check without having a ceiling placed upon the project.

I've addressed this with multiple attorneys that specialize in CEQA, and every one of them stated the city placed on me ridiculous timetables for completion (six to nine months) when a basic study should have taken no more than six to nine weeks. Also, the assistant city attorney insisted the city maintained full control of the study process—another conflict my attorneys specializing in CEQA stated was a ridiculous requirement placed on me. There was no reason why I couldn't have obtained my own consultant.

I'm not disagreeing with the fact that there were environmental requirements that needed to be looked into. But that occurs during the permitting process, after a lease has been approved by the city council. The issue only came up when Sky Trek's attorneys sent a letter on June 30, 2008 directly to the city regarding CEQA—days prior to my city council vote.

First of all the city never formally brought up CEQA

throughout the first eight months of this process. The only time it was mentioned to me was by Jerome Thiele, when I was in his office in May 2008. He told me, "Come outside, because I need to tell you something." As we stood outside the airport terminal, he said, "Sky Trek is going to bring up CEQA, do you know what that is? It's the law of delay."

Jerome Thiele insisted the city wasn't going to bring it up because, he felt, the planning department would have an exemption for the proposal. In fact Brad Wall, the city's lead agency contact and principal planner, signed a statement of exemption. That exemption was supposed to be filed with the Office of Planning and Research in Sacramento but never was. The manager of that office, Scott Morgan, reviewed the document after I faxed him a copy, and he stated this document was legitimate and he felt my particular proposal of an aboveground fuel-tank installation was exempt.

He was not happy, and he felt the City of Modesto may have violated the California Permit Streamlining Act. He thought many other airports in California had installed aboveground tanks without CEQA studies; he further stated that he felt the city couldn't pull me off the agenda from a council vote based on a CEQA study requirement. This is especially since city staff included the environmental specialist, the director of planning, and the city attorney signing off on the proposal to go forward to city council for the vote.

He felt there was "something not right about their process in doing that." He further stated "the proper procedure is to allow the process to go through the city council for the lease vote, then off to the permitting process to see if any environmental is necessary."

Of course the same letter in which Sky Trek's lawyer raised

this issue opened with a paragraph flexing their economic muscle.

The initial Airport Advisory Committee was chaired by John Rogers, the owner of Sky Trek, a multimillionaire and philanthropist in the Modesto community for many years. He was scathingly condescending, asking many questions regarding my proposal, and he even asked for the number of potential gallons I would expect. I didn't know at the time, and his response was "humor us, just give us something." The airport manager and other committee members were well aware this was a conflict of interest but allowed it to continue. In fact I asked the airport manager if this was an ethics violation. He knew about it and even mentioned that the committee members had attended ethics training recently.

During the second Airport Advisory Committee, John Rogers still chaired and was making comments throughout the process. When my proposal was up for vote, he said maybe "we should continue to look into this." But at that point, I made a comment that this was an ethics violation. It wasn't until then that the assistant city attorney, who was sitting next to him, stated, "Yeah, John, you need to stay out of this." If it weren't for my interjection, the city would've allowed him to continue to make decisions at the meeting.

The City of Modesto didn't know the process in which this proposal was supposed to go along. There were never established checklists or guidelines for me to follow. There were never any timelines in the beginning stages. Everything was done off the cuff. In fact I attached an e-mail between Jerome Thiele and the finance director, Wayne Padilla, dated February 14, 2008, and Wayne mentioned "there is no specific checklist for this kind of proposal."

It was all so apparent, especially when the competition (Sky Trek) realized this proposal was a reality and got their attorneys and consultants involved. In the letter dated May 15, 2008 from Jerome Thiele, there was a litany of onerous requirements they wanted. One of the items listed was the city's wanting to know about the financial outlook and business plan for the helicopter operation. This was irrelevant to the fuel-farm proposal.

Also listed was a one-year audited, consolidated financial statement. I contacted my CPA, Joe Mendez from the Kemper Group, and he said it was ludicrous to include that for a proposal like this. He continued: "There is really only one reason why they want you to do this—they don't want you to have it. This costs over $30,000 to do and is absolutely not necessary." Mr. Mendez called the finance director, Wayne Padilla, and said we weren't doing it.

Another requirement from the city was a personal financial statement. Including this made the document public. Going along with the process, I included it. Since then I have had several attorneys, consultants, and others state there are issues with including the personal financial statement.

The consultant who did my business plan and proposals included my personal financial statement in the business plan. But he stated there was a confidentiality request note to allow others to view it, and the intention was for this proposal only. We believe that wasn't the case. We feel there may have been a breach in that confidentiality—perhaps accidentally, perhaps intentionally.

1 approached Jerome Thiele about these onerous requirements, and he told me he was receiving a lot of pressure from Sky Trek and it "is what it is." I said to Jerome, "I feel like I'm

being discriminated against with all these requirements and delays. Are you telling me that if any tenant on this field wants to do a tenant improvement they have to do the same requirements you're setting forth with me? They have to go through the same process?"

Jerome Thiele's response was, "Sorry, Rick, that's how it is right now. I can't comment further."

Throughout the process the city used blatant issues and discriminating tactics. The city continued to hide behind the smokescreen of the CEQA being required, stating I didn't send the $5,000 deposit check to start the process. But it all falls back to delays. How long can Mr. Corbett go on before going away? They may have learned that by looking at my personal financial statement.

I've been approached by other tenants on the field and by the media, and I've been on the local news and the front page of the newspaper. All these parties came to the same conclusion: I have been wronged in this process; the City of Modesto, while saying it dealt with the process appropriately and the onus was on me to supply the $5,000 to do the study, behind the scenes ensured my proposal was to have multiple hurdles along the way.

The delays in this process defied belief. Every senior city staff official, including the city attorney, signed off on the proposal of my fuel farm. They all approved it to go forward for vote at the city council. In that agenda the statement of exemption was included. It wasn't until the letter from the attorney for Sky Trek that CEQA was required.

The city insisted they would get this rectified quickly, but the delays continued to happen. Dennis Turner promised an appraisal for my lease by July; I never received it. There was little to no communication for over a month, since my being pulled from the July city council meeting. It wasn't until around September that the city mentioned various costs for a CEQA to be done. Jerome Thiele at one point mentioned to me that I could obtain my own CEQA person. But later in the day, he called me back and stated the city would do the full inspection and have total control.

I was pulled from the July 8, 2008 city council meeting. It wasn't until September 8, 2008 that the city finally officially notified me that a CEQA was required and they had an estimate for a consultant. That letter contained a timeline of five weeks to complete. But the timeline Susana Wood, the city attorney, presented us in November showed over six months. Why such a large discrepancy between the studies?

My final word is that I'm sure there's a reason why there haven't been any fixed-based operators in the past eighteen years who have been successful in placing an additional fuel farm at Modesto Airport. It's the political clout and power that John Rogers and Sky Trek possess, and the effect that Mr. Rogers has on the City of Modesto.

I have been approached by many people who have told me I have gone farther than any other FBO in obtaining a fuel farm at Modesto airport. I have explained my position and the extensive hurdles I've had to endure to many people, including other FBO owners, the FAA, multiple attorneys, consultants, the media, and pilots from various aviation communities, and all have said the same thing: "What you have gone through is not right. This has to go public so it doesn't happen to someone else."

Chapter Fifteen
Would I Do It Again?

In a letter dated April 5, 2010, the FAA stated: "We find the Respondent—the City of Modesto, California—is not currently in violation of their Federal obligations… Accordingly, the above-referenced matter is dismissed."

This was definitely not what I wanted. The FAA, though not happy about the city's actions, had ruled:

> The Director finds that the [Modesto Airport] didn't violate Grant Assurance 22 Economic Nondiscrimination, because although there were delays in processing MFC's application for the above-ground fuel tanks, and the City is responsible for some of those delays, the Director is not persuaded that the actions amounted to an attempt to discriminate against MFC in the establishment of its fuel station;
>
> Grant Assurance 23 Exclusive Rights, because although the Airport was under pressure by its incumbent FBO to prevent fueling competition in the Airport, the city was moving forward to process MFC's application for a fuel station.

When you hear quacking and see a lot of feathers and webbed

footprints, you presume a duck is around. But since I couldn't produce a duck, the FAA rejected my claim.

Aside from this, the fact that under our judicial system the plaintiff in an action, like the prosecutor in a trial, has to prove his case, I consider the FAA decision to be wrong. But, and I almost hate to say this, I consider them to have been fair.

Final Thoughts

Looking back at this whole process, I think constantly that if I could have done something differently the whole thing may have had another outcome. I've consulted with several business colleagues and friends, and the general consensus is that I did everything I could do. Adding fuel to the business was a viable condition to continue the growth of the business, and the business plan that was reviewed by multiple sources to include the fuel distributer appeared to be sustainable.

But with all the legal wrangling involved, the downturn of the economy, the possible lack of disposable income, and the lack of commitment from the city, it was the final demise of the fueling idea—and the flight school itself—that bothered me.

Should we have added the helicopter operations so soon after the company Silver State had gone out of business? Yes and no. We created a mini-business plan to add the helicopter operation, to bring in the students who got left behind in their training when Silver State shut down. We thought, after meetings with former students, that we would gain approximately thirty students right upfront. With that information and the commitment we felt we had, we went ahead and started it up.

What about the Lincoln Airport Satellite operation, a

spinoff project attempt? Well, there wasn't much capital put out for that. We held meetings with local business folks and the airport manager, and the need for a quality flight school was deemed to be dire in that area. Cessna Pilot Centers verified that information and gave me the green light to go forward with it.

We did open houses, barbeques, and other gatherings to spark interest—but it was surprisingly a flop. Airplanes were sitting on the ramp in Modesto, not even flying, and what with positioning the aircraft to another location with information I was provided, we thought we would succeed. That simply wasn't the case.

There are other items I may have implemented that I couldn't complete. It was a nightmare—foreign students through the M1 visa program coupled with the FAR Part 141 school program. We had both working simultaneously for the approval process, and we came so close to getting those online. That may have been an additional revenue stream and would've been a great benefit and marketing tool outside the states.

So, would I try another investment in this type of industry? Maybe not the flight school side of the house. Aircraft charters or consulting would be more my style. I tried to do something to add to the community and to accomplish something from my experiences, but it wasn't successful. I need to focus and structure new investment ideas I can see five years down the road—anticipating the paths they can go down and the possible returns but also foreseeing the hurdles.

The flight school had a five-year plan, but I had no idea about the hurdles, hoops, and bureaucratic nightmares I would have to endure just to install a couple of fuel supply tanks.

Those barriers weren't part of the plan, and everyone on my team couldn't believe such actions were taken to prevent the success of the improvements. Oh, and how about that recession we went through in 2008, during my adventures with the fueling service and gas prices swelling to new highs?

I enjoy consulting with eager entrepreneurs about methods to get their businesses going. I have started three businesses but only had to close one. Not a bad success rate, though I could definitely improve. But even having a master's in business administration didn't prepare me for the enormous amount of practical experience I achieved by going for it!

I strongly encourage all those who've approached me about a business idea or opportunity in order to request my professional thoughts. I give both sides of the story to people who ask for my opinion, but I always end it by saying, "You never know unless you try. Give it a shot, but keep your eyes wide open!"

Appendix

-----Forwarded Message-----
From: *xxxxxxx@xxxxxxxx.net*
Sent: *Aug 20, 2008 9:43 AM*
To: *xxxxxx@xxxxx-xxxxx.com, xxxxx@xxxxx-xxxxx.com, xxxxxxx@xxxxxxxxxxxx.com,* Rich Pinnell *<xxxxxxx@xxxxxxx.com>*
Cc: Ralph Sauceda *<xxxxx@xxxxxxxxxxxxx.com>*, Tony Bustamante *<xxxxxxxxxxx@xxxxxxx.xx.com>*
Subject: *Fw: Cessna Pilot Center (CPC) Platinum Award for Modesto Flight Center*

Hello, folks!

Well...this was good news yesterday. Tried to send it to you, but wasn't sure if it went out. Figured I'd try again.

Anyway, MFC was selected for the highest award from Cessna Pilot Centers. This was a true surprise to me when I got the call. Our hard work has paid off to earn this prestigious award.

We can pass along to the city that our business is truly a nationally recognized business located in their community.

Thanks and have a great

day.
Rick

-----*Forwarded Message*-----
From: "Pitman, James" <xxxxxxxx@xxxxxx.xxxxxx.com>
Sent: Aug 19, 2008 4:15 PM
To: Richard Corbett <xxxxxxx@xxxxxxxxxxx.net>
Subject: Cessna Pilot Center (CPC) Platinum Award for Modesto Flight Center

To whom it may concern:

This letter is to inform you that Modesto Flight Center has been selected to receive the prestigious Platinum Award for their outstanding performance as a Cessna Pilot Center. This award will be presented at the Denver CPC seminar on September 22. Following the seminar, Cessna will issue a press release similar to the attached PDF file.
    Feel free to contact me for further information.
    Sincerely,
    Jim Pitman
    Regional Manager
    Cessna Pilot Centers
    Email: xxxxxxx@xxxxxx.xxxxx.com

CPC Platinum Award

The CPC Platinum Award is given to Cessna Pilot Centers that demonstrate outstanding performance. Benefits of receiving this award include:

- A high-quality plaque suitable for public display
- Recognition among peers (awards are presented at the CPC seminars).
- A Cessna press release
- Exposure on cessna.com/news Web site.
- General bragging rights (forward the Cessna press release to whomever you want).

Each regional manager is responsible for selecting CPCs in his or her territory to receive this award each year.

Prerequisites

To qualify for the CPC Platinum Award, CPCs must be in good standing with Cessna—following all requirements of the CPC agreement, which include:

- Having a qualifying airplane on the flight line or on order.
- Actively using and promoting the Cessna CBI curriculum.
- Having attended a CPC seminar within the previous two years (or be signed up for the next seminar).

Subjective Selection Criteria

The regional managers will use their judgment to select which CPCs receive the Platinum Award. In addition to the prerequisites listed above, decision factors include:

- Overall attitude of the CPC managers, instructors, and staff (Cessna team players).
- Effective use of the CPC and Cessna logos in advertising, signage, etc.
- Quality of relationship with CSTAR.
- Condition and upkeep of physical facilities.
- Efforts put into initiatives to promote flight training and the Cessna brand.

Citations

1. Eric Snyder, "The future for small airports? Still up in the air," *Nashville Business Journal*, January 8 2010, downloaded July 18, 2010 from http://www.bizjournals.com/nashville/stories/2010/01/11/story3.html.
2. Noelle Leavitt, "Rising fuels costs hurting general aviation reports," *Denver Business Journal*, May 16, 2008, downloaded July 19, 2010 from http://www.bizjournals.com/denver/stories/2008/05/19/story3.html?b=1211169600^1636523.
3. "SBA's Role," downloaded January 19, 2010 from http://www.sba.gov/financialassistance/borrowers/role/index.html.
4. Salerno, p. D4.
5. U.S. Department of Transportation, Federal Aviation Administration, "Subject: Exclusive Rights at Federally-Obligated Airports," January 4, 2007, AC No. 150/5190-6, p. 3-5.
6. FAA, p. 3.
7. Board of Supervisors, County of Humboldt, State of California, "Certified Copy of Portion of Proceedings," Meeting of December 6, 1994, Subject: NON-AGENDA ITEM—ARCATA-EUREKA AIRPORT—REPLACEMENT OF 50,000-GALLON AVIATION FUEL TANK,

downloaded from http://co.humboldt.ca.us/
board/agenda/questys/MG200008/AS200010/
AI200080/DO200081/BOSAgendaItem.pdf.

221

The building.

Sample fuel tanks.

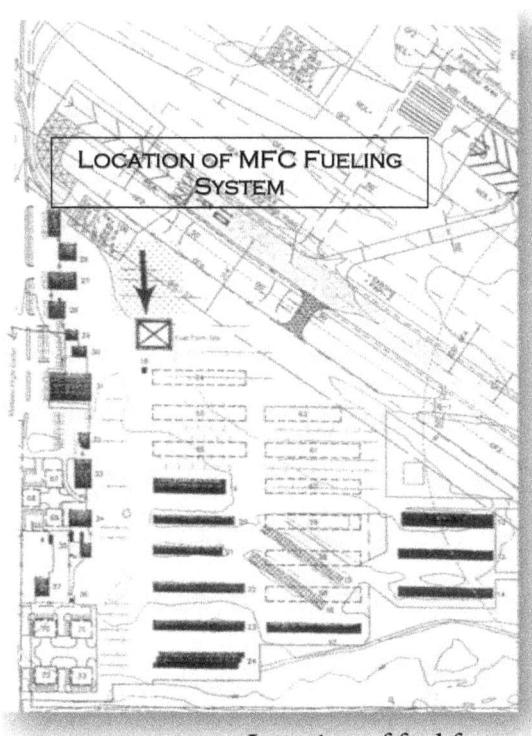
Location of fuel farm.

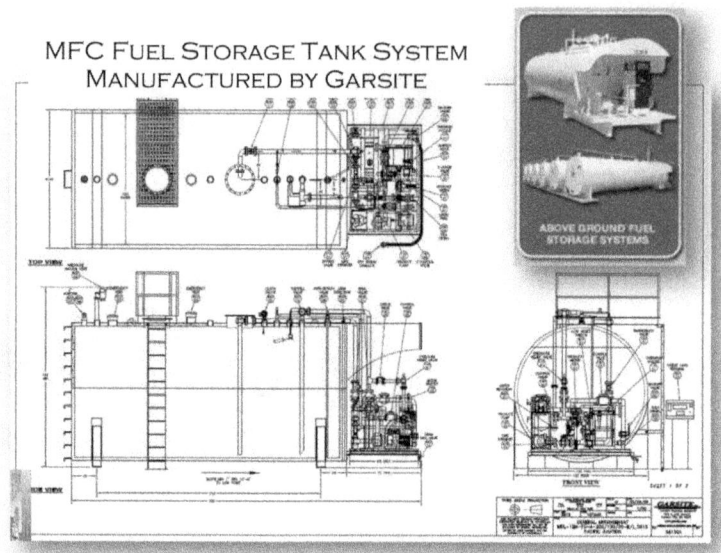

Schematic of fuel tank.

Modesto Airport Jet Fuel Statistics

Fuel Statistics	2005	2006	% inc/(dec)	2007	% inc/(dec)
Modesto Airport					
Jet-A Retail	812,712	814,880	0.3%	720,749	(12%)
Jet-A Airline	15,989	126,376	690.4%	244,151	52%
Totals	963,986	1,084,973		1,078,759	

Modesto Airport Avgas Statistics

Fuel Statistics	2005	2006	% inc/dec	2007	% inc/dec
Modesto Airport					
Avgas	135,285	143,717	6.2%	113,859	(21%)

www.ingramcontent.com/pod-product-compliance
Lightning Source LLC
Chambersburg PA
CBHW031345040426
42444CB00005B/198